ON THE APPROACH AND SCOPE OF THIS COLLECTION

Mindful Raft over Troubled Waters is a precise, simple and clear practical book on the development of non-judgmental, choiceless and insightful awareness that leads to the complete evolution of consciousness.

Dhiravamsa, International Vipassanā Meditation Master, Grand Canary Island, Spain, author of *Healing through Pure Mindfulness*, *Nirvana Upside Down*, *The Way of Non-attachment*, *The Middle Path of Life*, and *Una nueva visión del Budismo*.

If you're going to spend a year alone on an island, I would recommend you take *Mindful Raft over Troubled Waters* along with you. But if you are living the way most of us do, this book may be even more important for you to read. It has been so for me and still is.

Why? Because each time I read even a few lines, it has an immediate and magical effect of transporting me home to my true being. The simplicity and clarity of these words allow me to see things simply, as they are, without all the turmoil and dramas of my mind. So reading from this book helps me remember what's real — and forget all the rest.

Morgana Taylor, Totnes, Devon, UK.

These essays, like letters from a wise spiritual friend, emphasize the respect and kindness that are central to the heart's spiritual awakening.

Jack Kornfield, author of *Living Dharma*, *A Path With Heart*, *The Wise Heart*, and *A Lamp in the Darkness*.

To Vipassanā practice, certainly different approaches are possible and desirable; and certainly yours of "soft Vipassanā" can be helpful and effective. Those who are helped by it, may then feel encouraged to take up a stricter regimen.

Nyānaponika Mahāthera, Forest Hermitage, Kandy, Sri Lanka, author of *The Heart of Buddhist Meditation*.

The Venerable Mahāsī Sayādaw believes that your approach to Vipassanā Meditation is basically correct. You have done great work for the progress of the Vipassanā Meditation.

Mahāsī Sayādaw, Sāsana Yeiktha, Buddha Sāsana Nuggaha Organization, Rangoon, Myanmar (formerly Burma), and author of *Satipatthāna Vipassanā:*

Insight through Mindfulness, *The Progress of Insight* (with original Pāli text, *Visuddhi-ñāna-kathā*), and *Practical Insight Meditation*; in communication conveyed by his personal secretary, Dr. U Ba Glay.

Contemplation articulated, insight and concern expressed, it is as though getting in touch with a place within our own minds.

Tenzin Kachö Kiyosaki, Certified Hospice Chaplain, Buddhist Teacher, life coach, spiritual counselor, and author of *Precious Life: Three Points to Finding Happiness Even in Turbulent Times*. Ordained by H. H. the Dalai Lama and remained a Buddhist nun for 27 years.

It is indeed a remarkable contribution for those on the path of awakening and a good book for those who keep abreast of the Vipassanā technique and its application in daily life.

Ajit R. Telang, *Dilip*, vol. 27, no. 4 (quarterly journal published by Sudakshina Trust, Prabhadevi, Mumbai, India).

MINDFUL RAFT OVER TROUBLED WATERS

Also by Mitchell D. Ginsberg

Mind and Belief:
Psychological Ascription and the Concept of Belief

The Far Shore: Vipassanā, The Practice of Insight

The Inner Palace:
Mirrors of Psychospirituality
in Divine and Sacred Wisdom-Traditions

Calm, Clear, and Loving:
Soothing the Distressed Mind,
Healing the Wounded Heart

Peace and War and Peace:
The Heart in Transformation

Mindful Raft
over Troubled Waters

MITCHELL D. GINSBERG

Wisdom Moon Publishing
2015

MINDFUL RAFT OVER TROUBLED WATERS

Published by Wisdom Moon Publishing LLC
San Diego, CA, USA

Wisdom Moon™, the Wisdom Moon logo™, *Wisdom Moon Publishing*™, and *WMP*™ are trademarks of Wisdom Moon Publishing LLC.

www.WisdomMoonPublishing.com

Front cover artwork based on a scroll painting (1914) entitled *Tiānfēnghǎitāo* 天風海濤 *Winds of Heaven and Waves of the Sea* by Liú Lìqīng 劉立清 (1876-1920).

Back cover artwork digitally adapted from a 1976 photograph of the Reclining Buddha at the Ajanta Caves, taken by Jacques Rutzky.

ISBN 978-1-938459-49-8 (softcover, alk. paper)
ISBN 978-1-938459-51-1 (eBook)
LCCN 2015931458

CONTENTS

DEDICATED TO

the being aware
the trying to be aware
the being not quite ready to be aware
each of which we all have occasion to experience and learn from.

IN WARM GRATITUDE

To Dhiravamsa. To Yvonne and to Marie-Claude. To Loren Mosher and to R.D. Laing; to Professors K.R. Norman and Heinz Bechert. To Sam, Sylvia, and Ted. To Henry, Michael, and Judy. To Hans and Olga, Jacques and Orlie, Tew and Fizz, and Frank and Vivian. To Manfred, Paul, Jo, Brenda, and Ed. To Bob, Peter, Roland, Charles, and Jean-Pierre. And to Wendy, Hrjjayā, and Fanny.

IN ACKNOWLEDGMENT

of all who have taught and inspired me, of those who have encouraged me in the project of this book, especially of Peter, whose acute and sensitive reading of an earlier draft of this book has improved its flow, of Jo for the aesthetics of the line drawing of the Reclining Buddha, of Paritta, Noy, and the Ven. Pra Kru Lom for the elegant classical Thai calligraphy, of Jacques for his exquisitely clear, hand-held time-exposure photograph of the Reclining Buddha, offered for use on the cover of this book, and of Dhiravamsa, Wendy, and Tew, each of whom opened the right door at the right time.

A WORD TO THE READER

If you're going to spend a year alone on an island, I would recommend you take *Mindful Raft over Troubled Waters* along with you. But if you are living the way most of us do, this book may be even more important for you to read. It has been so for me and still is.

Why? Because each time I read even a few lines, it has an immediate and magical effect of transporting me home to my true being. The simplicity and clarity of these words allow me to see things simply, as they are, without all the turmoil and dramas of my mind. So reading from this book helps me remember what's real — and forget all the rest.

As I return to the natural state of simply seeing — seeing what is — I am immersed in peace, nothing else matters, everything is perfect just as it is. It is then I can let go and, in a flash, I'm there — reality.

Morgana Taylor
Totnes, Devon, England

❀ ☙ 🙐 ♥ ❀ ☙ 🙐 ♥ ❀ ☙ 🙐 ♥ ❀ ☙ 🙐 ♥

PREFACE

The mindful journey of this raft over troubled waters is to the far shore, itself representing a consciousness that can see our realities clearly and with deep loving-kindness, free of the distortions and reactivity that are our more usual human lot.

This is a space of understanding, appreciation, and caring good-will for all beings, a space of calm and well being, whose mark is wisdom, the marriage or skillful integration of compassion and insight.

In short, this is where the awakened mind, with full caring and deep understanding for other sentient beings and for oneself, can operate effectively and helpfully.

Mindful Raft over Troubled Waters describes and illustrates the path to developing this transformed consciousness in a wide range of human experiences. It presents the thinking and feeling processes in ways that allow us non-judgmental insight into the roots of our various states of mind, trains of thought, preferences, and consequent intentions and actions that together all lead us in one direction or another in our lives.

Such an awareness allows us to cultivate a compassionate appreciation of ourselves and others, a gentle understanding of the difficulties, challenges, and limitations we all live through, trying to deal with our life situations, our desire for perfection balanced by a recognition that good enough may be better than perfect ("cutting some slack" for ourselves and others, as some say).

This compassionate understanding, this deep appreciation, has been called wisdom and is something that many have searched for through the millennia. The path itself is now often referred to as mindfulness, or mindfulness practice, which is gaining in fame and respect; here is an opportunity to see its actual operation and application to a wide variety of specific life situations, to illustrate this practice in action.

This consciousness, which has undergone a very powerful transformation, is cultivated through the ongoing, systematic application of mindfulness to our moment-to-moment experience.

Such mindfulness allows an ongoing recognition of what is actually happening in our life. Here, we come to see through all of our judgments (and our moralizing and evaluating) to our actual experiences, the ways in which we are impacted by them, and the processes of our mind in attempting to deal with these life situations.

How we communicate, which forms our communications take or utilize, can vary widely from context to context. Here, to express one practical consideration as an example of this general concern, I cannot communicate by this or any other book what can only be communicated in person. Still, there is *something* I feel I can get across through writing, and I have an interest here in trying. This endeavor will be greatly helped by earnest interest and a clear awareness of what I want to express to you, on my part, and an openness on your part to hear what I have to say and to see how it touches you personally.

In this book, of course, what I put into black-and-white print represents living speech. I could have tried a recording instead of a book. But I have not, and so, I ask you to *listen* to what you see. If you do not hear what I am saying, I suggest that you read aloud — and see if it really doesn't talk to you.

My getting these pieces down has been easy at times, at times demanding; done sometimes in a serious mood and sometimes in a playful one, but always as a labor of love. Friends who have become acquainted with these writings tell me that they find value for themselves in them. Perhaps these pieces will touch you, too.

I find a deep poetry in clear awareness. I see that there is a power in this sort of awareness, a power to lead us to a heartfelt appreciation of life. Some might speak here of the awe we feel before what strikes us as divine or mysterious; I simply want to share some of my experience and observations with you in a way which may help you in looking at how your life is coming along and in realizing how we either move along with changing reality or work towards what we feel to be valuable in the context of life's flow. Insight here, as elsewhere, is a product of looking and so seeing.

This watchful attitude towards life was systematized long ago by the Buddha as the practice of mindfulness (sati-paṭṭhāna). As this practice has as its fruit the arising of insight into life, it has also been called vipassanā or, more fully, vipassanā bhāvanā (insight meditation).

A number of chapters here took their first form in the late 1970s and early 1980s as transcripts (notes written from memory) from various talks I gave while leading vipassanā meditation retreat courses and workshops in England, France, Norway, and the United States; others began as drafts of letters exchanged with friends and students; a number of pages were first simply jotted-down ideas and observations on my own when in a meditative mood; still others have been added in a variety of contexts in the years and decades that have followed.

Through this expanse of time, this evolving collection was shown to a number of individuals involved in the Buddhist tradition; some of their remarks and reviews are presented in the first pages of this book.

The contents have been entirely reviewed and freshly formatted for this publication; many chapters have been revised and rephrased from earlier versions, hopefully having the text come closer now to what I would like to communicate at this time, in a way that is clearer, more flowing, more explicit, more grounded, and more convincing.

These pieces variously illustrate sati-paṭṭhāna as the investigation into the processes of consciousness founded on an open mindfulness.

The coming to be familiar with this *accepting* awareness, an awareness that rests on a vast good will (a caring, loving attitude), is at the same time very acute and crisp in its perception; it occurs in many ways and is spurred on by the widest of contexts. We do not have to sit motionless in seated meditation to have this frame of mind-and-heart strengthen. This collection offers one such context, from beginning to end, from the words to Ms. Kitty to the question about the mouse.

I offer this collection under the title *Mindful Raft over Troubled Waters* to those of you who are on the path of self-discovery and on the path of opening to relationship with others. It does not matter if you are or are not already acquainted with Buddhist Insight (Vipassanā) Meditation, or with Buddhist psychology and its ways of conceptualizing. The far shore as a frame of consciousness is certainly not limited to those who see themselves as Buddhists. Still, some of these writings will be especially pertinent to those have attended vipassanā meditation retreat courses and to their continuing practice. For general interest, a list of some contact addresses of centers is given, in the section toward the end of this book, Meditation Centers.

A few terms are occasionally used here that may not be familiar to you. A Glossary at the back of this book gives an idea of what these various terms mean: from some possibly familiar to you such as the Buddha, dharma, bodhisattva, and dukkha, to some lesser-known such as anupassanā, sādhu, and lokuttarasīla.

A glance at the titles in the Table of Contents gives a feeling for the range of topics included. Some of the writings focus on issues in the practice of open mindfulness. *I find that people with no familiarity in the Buddhist tradition, either practical or theoretical, follow these writings with ease. There is nothing esoteric here.*

This book is a gathering together of reflections on, and descriptions of, our various moments of experience that can be appreciated more fully if considered in this meditatively attentive way. In this collection you will find Instructive Dharma, an explanation of the Dharma as the matrix of the vipassanā practice, perspective, and tradition; and also, Descriptive Dharma, an illustration of Dharma as the various evolving realities within the domain of mindfulness practice. Pieces with a manifestly Instructive Dharma aspect include Vipassanā in Munich, Spiritual development, Mind clouds, and The past.

The Space of Silence

To orient mindfulness practice in a larger context here, the world of meditation includes many varied activities and fundamental understandings of the world. There is, for example, a large group of meditation traditions and practices that involve chanting, telling of stories, or repeating of ritual texts, and movements of the body, whether rocking or walking about in some particular sequence, as a dance either choreographed or spontaneous, with rhythms perhaps marked by clapping or percussion instruments of various sorts, and perhaps also with the expression of sounds of intense experience, for example, sounds of joy, or ecstasy, or perhaps of somber repentance, grief, or woefulness.

Considering insight meditation, or mindfulness practice, we may appreciate that this meditation practice shares some similarity with a wide variety of meditation practices around the world in which there is stillness and quiet, both in body and speech. That is, if we think of monks, hermits, and other serious meditators from various traditions, we can easily imagine them still, seated, not talking at all, perhaps for extended periods of time measurable in days or even in years.

Staying with meditation practices of stillness and silence, while these may look the same in these ways to the outsider observing the meditators, what is going on in the minds of the various meditators can vary greatly. There may be rehearsals of significant religious scenes and related considerations including the spiritual morale to be drawn and emphasized, there may be repetitions of important declarations or of special sounds, there may be much self-questioning and self-criticism, this last being much more in the Western (or Eurocentric) understanding of what meditation is all about, a kind of deep contemplation or rumination.

In meditation, we may experience not only external silence, where we do not make any noises at all, but also internal silence, a time or a space where we are not taken up by long trains of thought or of complex fantasies, where we are even free of thinking and especially free of judgmental evaluations of ourselves or of others.

This silence is a space where we can experience an alternative to the ongoing wheel of thinking, planning, doing, and interacting, of our regular activities making ourselves busy, where we can then experience the deep calm that is within our consciousness, which is in a sense the stage or backdrop for whatever comes onstage to capture our attention.

This mention of the Space of Silence is to add one more feature of mindfulness, as further background for our considerations here and throughout this book with its many illustrations of mindfulness meditation in actual practice.

The Taste of Mindfulness in Practice

To give a sense of what consciousness is like when mindfulness is active, grounded and ongoing, we may make apply a metaphor used by the Buddha in speaking of the ocean, which has one taste, that of saltiness. Similarly, we may continue here, the taste of a consciousness brought to calm resolution and radiating good will is one that has the taste of freedom, of relaxation, of clear awareness, of seeing without judging, of effortless appreciation of the situation. The many examples in this book of specific investigations using mindfulness and of the awareness that that practice brings, hint at this taste. Read on for more!

Mindful Raft over Troubled Waters is not meant to be a primer in Buddhist psychology, in Buddhism, or, more specifically, in vipassanā meditation (also called the cultivation of insight, mindfulness practice, mindfulness-insight meditation). Following the Glossary is a list of some available books that already fulfill such a function.

Given that, this may be a good place to mention that in one of the books listed in the Glossary is an in-depth, well-organized discussion of vipassanā meditation, placing it in its fuller originally-Buddhist context, presenting its theoretical framework, its specific recommendations in practice, and its ultimate purpose: This is Chapter 10 (entitled "The Liberating Power of Mindfulness"), in M. Ginsberg, *Calm, Clear, and Loving: Soothing the Distressed Mind, Healing the Wounded Heart* (Second edition, 2012), pp. 164-173.

Uparujjhati uddhaccaṃ
kukkuccaṃ parihīyati
cetanā cetanā yeva
ariyaṃ saccaṃ sukhaṃ mano.

Anattā khalu saṅkappā
suñño so paccayāsayo
ānāpāno va kāyamhi
annaṃ kho dhammapīti me.

อุปรุชฌติ   อุทธจฺจํ
กุกฺกุจฺจํ   ปริหียติ
เจตนา   เจตนา   เยว
อริยํ   สจฺจํ   สุขํ   มโน

อนตฺตา   ขลุ   สงฺกปฺปา
สุญฺโญ   โส   ปจฺจยาสโย
อานาปาโน   ว   กายมฺหิ
อนฺนงฺโข   ธมฺมปีติ   เม

उपरज्झति उद्धच्चं ।
कुक्कुच्चं परिहीयति ॥
चेतना चेतनायेव ।
अरियं सच्चं सुखं मनो ॥

अनत्ता खलु सङ्खप्पा ।
सङ्खतो अप उपच्चयामयो ॥
आनापानी व कायम्हि ।
अम्बं खो धम्मपीति मे ॥

Restlessness ceases
remorse is abandoned
thinking is just thinking;
truth is noble — the heart's at ease.

Plans surely have no owner
quite empty is that realm of conditioning
in the body there is breathing, in and out —
the drink of *dhamma* is indeed my nourishment.

CONVERSATION

Etadatthā kathā, etadatthā mantaṇa, etadatthā upanisā, etadatthā sotāvadhānaṃ yad idaṃ anupādā cittassa vimokkho 'ti.

Conversation is for this purpose, consultation is for this purpose, getting close is for this purpose, listening is for this purpose — for the clinging-free liberation of consciousness.

Vinaya V.164.

Sakalameva hidaṃ ānanda brahmacariyaṃ, yadidaṃ kalyāṇamittatā kalyāṇasahāyatā kalyāṇasampavaṅkatā.

Truly, the entire spiritual life, Ananda, is this — an encouraging friendship, an encouraging companionship, an encouraging intimacy.*

Samyutta-nikāya I.87-88.

To extend sincere love to one you cherish is worthwhile to each of them, the giver and receiver.

Samuel L. Ginsberg (1906-1999), May 25, 1976.

* The word translated as "encouraging" here, *kalyāṇa*, means beautiful, agreeable, good, noble, generous, excellent, beneficial, virtuous, auspicious, that which encourages, that which inspires; a *kalyāṇa mitta* (*mitta* means friend) — in the Theravada Buddhist Tradition, a meditation teacher — is a good friend, a virtuous friend, a friend (in this Buddhist context) who inspires and encourages us in our process of coming to awakening and freedom.

ON THE FAR SHORE

Let go the future.
Let go the past.
Let go the present.
Be on the far shore.

The Buddha
Dhammapāda 348

MINDFUL RAFT OVER TROUBLED WATERS

TO MS. KITTY

Petted

the cat purrs contentedly

Pushed away
by firm hand
by gruff voice

she turns away, then looks back
turns around and walks off
to the next reality
easily
letting go of unwelcoming spaces.

And you?

VIPASSANĀ IN MUNICH

The practice of vipassanā meditation was first taught by the Buddha. It consists in the open attentiveness to what we experience. In this way we come to know and appreciate reality as it is, not as our ideas tell us it must be. Through mindfulness comes insight (vipassanā).

Traditionally, the practice is done in sitting, standing, and in walking postures. In our practice we go deeply into our experience, using the discipline of mindful silence to help us become more sensitive to how we in fact respond to what life actually offers us, and to be more in touch with ourselves on the physical, emotional, mental, and spiritual levels, within the limits of our conditioning, and beyond.

For sitting meditation, we have found that sitting practice with the eyes closed and for a period of about one hour allows our more profound energies to come to the surface for us to experience fully. This differs somewhat from certain other meditation traditions such as Rinzai Zen which uses eyes-open sitting for shorter periods of time.

In addition to this core of sitting practice, we also use various body-oriented exercises including free movement, dancing and perhaps shaking to music, and so forth. We are aware that various deep psychological patterns are held in the body itself, and by allowing the body to work directly with these holding or storage areas, the freeing up of these residues from the past is accelerated. (To put this into traditional terms, this is the work of burning karma.)

> For use in an announcement of a
> workshop to be held with the
> Munich group.

PICK ONE TECHNIQUE AND STICK TO IT

Let's not get lost in defining the word technique, and after that in determining whether vipassanā meditation is a technique, *but*: what sort of attitude is being advocated when we are told to pick one technique and stick to it? And what is happening when we ourselves decide to follow one technique exclusively?

If we look, we may experience fear and reluctance: *fear* that some satisfying state we have attained might be lost, or that a direction of change we've liked might be cut off, and *reluctance* to go beyond what we are content with by trying something new.

All of this frequently leads to a narrowing down, a closing off, a rigidifying. This rigidifying out of fear may also lead on a grander scale to sectarianism. Have you ever heard these isolationist words?

"We Mahāyānists, on the other hand, . . ."
"The Adamantine Teaching, which is supreme, . . ."
"The purity of the U Ba Khin Tradition . . ."
"Those pagan heretics . . ."
"Death to all infidels . . ."

All this is simply more of what we call the net of views, the trap of views, the thicket of views, the clinging to views.

In this we see a self-limiting tendency, a defensive attitude towards, or rather *against*, an unknown future reality, a desire to keep things (onflowing reality) under our control.

We can appreciate our satisfaction, our contentment, our happiness, our joy, without freezing into immobility, without attempting to ward off change. (*Could* change be warded off?) But perhaps we will see such a futile attempt arise. If so, maybe we see its basis and get a perspective on it all, so that when this attempt to ward off change does ultimately fail, we are not spun into turmoil.

At each point in the flow of life, we may see preferences being formulated for what the next moments will be like. Then we may see these preferences channeling our energies. And perhaps once in a while we will begin noticing an occasional neutrality towards the next moments: a full openness, a deep interest in what they will be, in what they are, not for what they do for us or against us, but simply because they are. This is like scientific curiosity, with heart.

3

ALL PATHS

All path which lead inwards and onwards
      In tenderness and in love
Surely show their worth.

THE FAR SHORE'S UNDER YOUR FEET

We may feel some sort of progress or advancement while we are at a meditation retreat: we may have seen some difficulty for us come up, and seen it disappear. This may be followed by the idea that this difficulty will never again be experienced. That *would* indeed be nice, wouldn't it?

So what, then, if it does arise again at some later time? Maybe you will see it on your very first day out of the retreat setting! What then?

If we let the difficulty appear again, rather than thinking it won't, and resisting it when it does, we can look further into a process that began here at the retreat, to see it end, or, if it doesn't end, to see how it continues or evolves. In either case, we let it flow through and then we are clear of it.

We can use a retreat situation as an environment where a clearing out of ourselves can take place. And we can use all of life that way; all of life can be a retreat. But it's a retreat in the world. All that is needed is the same attitude that is nurtured in a retreat setting.

This is not in the sense of having rules about how to behave: sometimes we go to a retreat and the people there have some suggestions for us about how to act during the retreat. When we go out into the world after the retreat ends, we might think that the essence of the retreat is following certain rules.

With vipassanā there is also a morality or way of right acting. Now, the way of right acting that comes from vipassanā does not come through following rules. The way of right acting through vipassanā is seeing what is to be done. If we are driving down the street and we see a car stop in front of us, we don't need a rule, "Stop when the car in front of you stops." With insight we see that there is a car stopped in front of us.

And in general, in this path, we see the right action not through a rule, but by seeing what the reality is. Appreciating the reality, we see how things are going. We act in accordance with what is appropriate to the reality. That is a kind of morality, but a morality without rules.

5

We don't need rules about how to retain what we have learned during this retreat, about how to keep our mindfulness from diminishing when we leave the retreat setting. To start with, though, we can already see here a desire to have something continue, which feels right to us at the present moment. Or maybe we feel desperation about it — not merely a desire. Well then, the way we have mindfulness continue after the retreat is to continue being mindful: to keep breathing after the retreat, we just keep breathing. We don't need a rule: First there is an in-breath and then an out-breath, and we do it in that order, and continue doing it. No: we just keep on breathing. And we just keep on being mindful.

Certainly the experience outside the retreat will be different from the experience within the retreat. Even the experience within the retreat is different from the experience within the retreat: how it is now is different from how it was ten minutes ago. What you are seeing now is different from what you were seeing ten minutes ago. How your body feels now is different. So that will be the same; it will be different. It'll be different when you leave the retreat. So there may be more noise that you hear. There may be more interpersonal contact with other people. There may be more feeling of practical pressures: pressure to do this, pressure to do that.

Maybe you will be seeing a different reality. Then you will have the chance to learn more and more about yourself. By putting yourself into more and more contexts, you have a lot of lessons to learn from. We can treat reality as something that gives us problems and hassles, and something to be borne, some burden we have to carry, or some drudgery that we have to get through. Or we can treat reality as something to learn about, just to see what it is: that is mastering the mystery of Māyā. Until Māyā is mastered, it is reality that has the power to delude us, since we are continually misinterpreting it. Māyā is mastered just by our seeing into Māyā, by appreciating all the little realities that are created, all the different experiences that we come through.

We can enjoy Māyā. We can understand it, and then we aren't deluded by it. We can appreciate what's happening. Then Māyā is simply samsāra, the on-going flow, or the circle or cycle of life. We look into samsāra, appreciate it, and then it is no longer Māyā for us.

When we appreciate it fully — this is being in a nirvanic state, in nibbāna. In Buddhist terms, we can say that samsāra is nirvāṇa.

We can talk of crossing over to the far bank. But we have to understand what the far bank is. The far bank isn't separate from samsāra. The far bank is seeing through samsāra so that it is no longer illusion to us, no longer Māyā to us.

When we see all of our reality for what it is, when we allow each experience to be just what it is, without reading all sorts of interpretations into it, then we are already on the other shore. Crossing the stream of samsāra is a matter of changing our experience of each moment of consciousness by allowing it to be just as it is. You don't have to travel anywhere to get to the far shore: the far shore's under your feet.

So we see beyond this shore and that shore. We're in samsāra but not of it: we simply experience the world of phenomena, and so we're experiencing samsāra, but not being carried away by it, not being deluded by it. When we go back into our "normal" or "real" life after a retreat, there is a chance to experience more of that, to learn more about that.

So we see if we enjoy life or if it pains us. Sometimes there will be pain. There is no guarantee that it will be painless along the way. We don't have an expectation of its being painless, or of its being painful. We just see what it is. If it's painless now, we enjoy its painlessness. But when there is pain, when there is some kind of a problem, we can look at it, we can see it. Then we can continue taking it all in stride. We don't let it build and build that way until it ends by being overpowering.

This is treating life not as a burden to be borne for a while, until death. We don't live life just waiting for death. That is not the aim of life, or the goal of life, even though it might be the end of life. We are just living and experiencing, learning, seeing what's happening, having insight, having vipassanā into the way things really are, cultivating insight and growing through insight. That's vipassanā living, living a meditative life.

7

COMPASSIONATE INSIGHT

On the far shore, there is a calm clarity that can feel very solid, easy, grounded, unshakable. We may have heard of the establishing of an unshakable base, that is not agitated or reactive or confused about whatever is arising in our experience, about whatever is happening in the life situation we find ourselves in at the time.

With the grounded tranquility, it is much easier to see exactly what is going on and what is important for each person we interact with. We can see what others' concerns, worries, irritations, hopes, fears, and so forth are all about, and how these are leading to the various thoughts, words, and actions of those around us.

When we can come to appreciate the underlining discomfort, agitation, or torment (dukkha) that is bothering the other person, we can naturally, effortlessly, feel the arising of a wish that that person be at peace and safety and well being.

And in this, we can observe the operation of compassionate insight, the skillful integration of compassion and insight, the harmonious marriage of deep wisdom and resonant loving kindness and on a firm foundation of unshakable tranquility.

THE BUDDHIST PEACOCK

When we think of a peacock, in our Western culture, we think of someone who is full of himself, who is perhaps a braggart, who shows off what he takes to be his best, most attractive or admirable features, whether he thinks of these as his physical form, his wealth, his accomplishments, his property, or anything that he thinks might attract admiration and desire, with him as the desired object.

This is our image of the peacock as a bird that flaunts its wonderfully brilliant plumage as part of a mating ritual.

In Buddhism, there is another understanding of the peacock.

While it is clear that the peacock's tail features are a sight to behold, what Buddhists such as the Indic poets Dharmarakṣita and Atiśa (or Dharmarakshita and Atisha), from about a millennium ago, have come to understand is that the peacock represents a living being who is capable of surviving a meal of berries that will kill other birds. In fact, the bird is said not only to survive the ingestion of these poisonous berries, but, in fact, to be nourished by them.

The peacock in Buddhist literature ingests and digests the nutrition found in these berries, without succumbing to the poisons it holds for other birds.

What does this have to do with us? Certainly we are not peacocks. Of course, the story is taken as a metaphor for us to make use of. The idea in Buddhism here is that we can approach what is thought of as noxious, as troublesome, as disturbing, as a torment to avoid, and to make use of it to transform our consciousness quite profoundly, arriving at a great compassion, all as part of our moving toward the far shore.

What does this digestion amount to and how does it work? We may alternatively ask the question, what is the nutrition to be obtained from these "berries" that we think of as the poisons of life? And what does the digestion and integration of these poisons into our psyche amount to? What is this profound transformation of our very consciousness? How can we recognize it? And, perhaps even better, how can we anticipate it and encourage it?

If we remain attentive to what the flavor of our experience is like, what our frame of mind is like, we will certainly notice variations, our experience being part of the world of impermanence, anicca. Within these variations, we can note which moments of experience tend to draw us to them and which tend to repel us, to push us away, or to have us instinctively turn away or try to avoid them if at all possible.

These disturbing, irritating, agitating, or frightening moments of experience are what would count as berries in this extended metaphor. We can rather easily notice them as they first appear in our experience.

We can next notice how we understand or interpret the experience; we can see the significance or meaning that we give to ourselves. If we take the experience to indicate a problem, there is something we take to be somehow detrimental to us or to something in our personal world. We can notice and see all of this if we keep paying attention rather than turning away or in some way distracting ourselves from the situation.

The peacock here will not distract itself, will not react trying to avoid what is unpleasant, or what it suspects will end up being unpleasant. It will allow its energy and attention to go into seeing the particulars of the situation.

Whatever the particulars, we will notice ways in which we have tried to avoid this or that "berry" and with that, have been living a reactive life.

If we can begin to look at this process of avoidance, to start with, we may at first see that we are putting energy and thinking into our importantly limited and narrow perspective or point of view here, thereby creating a bias, which is always a distortion, focusing on one part of a greater story and minimizing or disregarding other parts.

Instead of this, if we can slow down this process, and reach a state of tranquility, of calm equanimity, we may begin to see things in a larger framework, seeing perhaps the interactions of the various individuals involved in the situation, and how each is working to achieve some goal or to avoid some situation felt to be deleterious.

We may begin to understand the workings of each individual in the situation and the working of the worries, fears, angers, hopes, and such of each. Here we have a compassionate appreciation of each person and a clear understanding of the entirety of the situation, acting together in an effortless flow of caring action. And in this, we can observe the operation of what some call compassionate insight, the skillful integration of compassion and insight, the harmonious marriage of deep wisdom and resonant loving kindness and on a firm foundation of unshakable tranquility.

We return to this topic below in the chapter "Turning poison into nectar" (pages 96-97).

SPIRITUAL DEVELOPMENT

Where are we going on this spiritual trip? Is it just more heavy luggage in a journey already replete with burdens?

Have we once again given up our ability to judge for ourselves, turning away from the problems and complications of life with some predigested "truth"?

So we're looking for something. This means we can see dissatisfaction, an unacceptable situation, an unacceptable experience. We may feel an emptiness in the way things are, a desire to make things better, a desire to improve ourselves. And what do we imagine as a solution to this dissatisfaction?

We may look to certain people as models: We hear of someone who is so "spiritually developed" that when he sits in meditation, a light is visible glowing forth from him. Or of another who has such "spiritual powers" that a large pin stuck in a cheek causes no pain.

Are *you* that developed? And is this really the something extra you want from life? Is *this* what "higher development" is aimed at? Does *your* deepest problem come because your aura isn't the right color?

Let's get back to earth. Here we are. Each day our time and energy flow onwards. Does it feel smooth, comfortable, acceptable? Is it sometimes rough going, painful, unacceptable? Is the flow more like a whirlpool than a brook?

If we inspect our life situation more deeply than by merely noting each separate instant of consciousness by itself, we begin to see inter-relations and patterns. Some of these involve great pain. Many show how we repeatedly resist the ongoing flow of reality, or, at least, attempt to channel it according to desires that are constantly arising.

We can appreciate this capacity to gain insight into our various ways of living in the world, and continue seeing more and more deeply how we are going through life. Or, we may find ourselves getting entangled in our *thinking* about how we are going through life; perhaps our mind will take a philosophical bent and come up with the cavalier idea that it's all illusion, all māyā. But, all we need is a little deep pain to have us recover our senses.

Back with our senses, what we experience is not this or that conception of how reality *ought* to be, but the particulars of our situation as humans in this time and space. When we arise in the morning, we feel hunger in our bellies. When we feel good-willed love from others, we feel a new, special energy. When we see another in distress, we know that sadness, or wonder what it must really feel like. When we are tired, we want to rest. When our environment is beautiful, we are at peace. (Salvador Dali once said that the soul is a state of the landscape.)

The most spiritual life is the most mundane. (Put in a Buddhist way, nirvāna is samsāra.) The role of spiritual development is in the *active* liberation of our limited energies from all those pain-producing, self-constricting and inter-personally poisonous channels it is repeatedly flowing into.

We can get on with this liberation without becoming passive through fear of acting. And without beclouding any of our mind's natural crisp clarity.

When we truly allow every bit of reality to show itself to us, we allow in not only what we feel is good, or proper, or "spiritually developed," but anything and everything. Then we can learn from life in all it fullness. We appreciate the idea that our eyes and our heart will be present at *all* times (1 Kings 9:3).

When we become open to learn from life in all its fullness, we are alive to learning more and more deeply how our lives and how our relationships in the world are coming along. We are travelling on, becoming intimately aware of how life works. This is how we carry on. "A man cannot know himself better than by attending to the feelings of his heart and to his external actions," wrote Boswell in 1762.

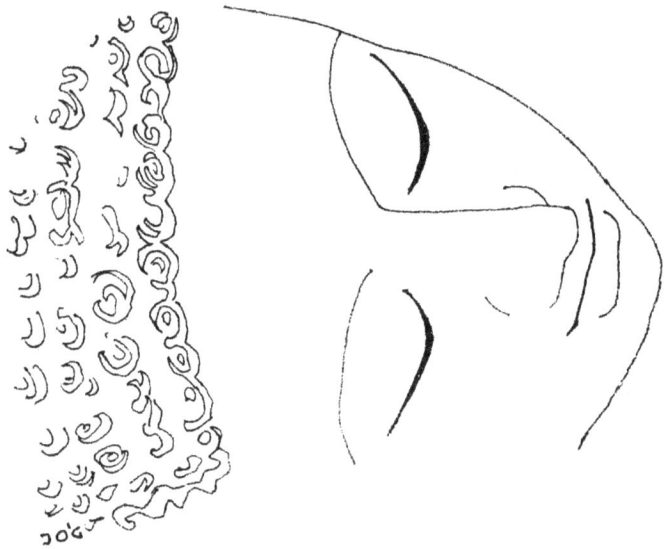

LOVE AND RESPECT

We may say that what is really important in life is love, pronounced softly and full of vibrancy in our voice, and we may feel this to be oh so true. And yet we may notice our energies going into concerns about respect.

When we look at these two, at love and at respect, it is clear that they are miles, no, worlds apart. The deep contentment and joy to be alive which are born of love just aren't generated by respect.

Respect focuses on identity, especially on socially definable identity. It has in its domain the world of credentials: "I did this." "I've associated with these great people." "I was honored by this significant group." "I've been invited to this or that important occasion."

Respect brings about comparison, evaluating personal worth, competition between people, pride and shame.

It is a losing game. Within its structure, its limits, its rules, even when we are "winning," we are only standing on the sandy ground of social fictions. We get our support from the recognition of others, and so we lean heavily. This makes us very unstable, unsure, and ill at ease.

And, when within its structure we are "losing," we do not even have the little strength that being respected occasionally brings us by giving us some confidence. But we do have true self-disrespect: We don't like ourselves; or rather, we don't like our socially-known image. And we don't really look at ourselves (dis-re-spect: the lack of seeing ourselves).

So what, then, if we say and feel that love is what is really important in life! For, in spite of how we feel about love, we may have a deep stake in respect, in what it brings to us, especially in the initial feeling of satisfaction and superficial level of acceptance, or in its various forms of power.

The way of love is not the way of power. If we long for what the way of love involves but march down the way of power, our longings here will never be fulfilled.

We could see years if not lifetimes of frustration arising out of such a mischanneling of life's precious energies.

So it is important for us to appreciate what we experience as valuable, and what we *do*. If these are not in harmony, as when we feel the value of love and yet strive for power and distancing respect, we can look carefully to appreciate how this disharmony arises.

Perhaps we have a confusion. Maybe we equate love with respect. Once, feeling love and friendship and goodwill for her, I hugged a seven-year-old friend of mine. She looked at me with some puzzlement and asked, "What did I do that you liked, Mitchell?" Perhaps in her experience, expressions of love were typically connected with approval of some form. So we may be far from the experience of love as just love, and have familiarity mostly with love for deeds done or accomplishments accomplished. Love becomes just one more form of payment to a capitalist mentality.

Such a confusion is not that uncommon. Such a confusion has powerful consequences. Such a confusion can be overcome by appreciating these consequences.

The disharmony may have other roots. When you next notice such a disharmony, what will *its* basis be? Or perhaps you will just notice, uninterruptedly, full harmony in your present life!

THE FLOWER

The flower
       wide-open to the warming sun
Shuts up tight
       against the cold-night wind.

Karuṇa-pati asks: is one less beautiful than the other?

The Commentary says at this point: the flower is our tender heart.

THE DISCOURSE ON FREEDOM THROUGH
GOOD COMPANIONSHIP

My friends Michael and Judy were going to celebrate their union through a Sufi wedding ceremony, atop Mount Tamalpais. I was asked to read a Buddhist selection as part of that Universal-Worship ceremony. I looked for something not syrupy sweet, as I had the feeling that there would be enough of that without my contribution. I found an inappropriate word by Shantideva advising against relating to immature spirits (bālajana — or, fools, as some translate it), and one by D. H. Lawrence offering in a poem the idea of taking the sun from one another and leaving the valueless rest. Michael said the selection should be *obviously* Buddhist. So I put what I felt worthwhile and relevant to say to them in the form and style of a traditional Pāli sutta. Michael asked if there was a mention of bodhisattvas and such, and so I added an uncharacteristic sprinkle of such beings among those present to hear the discourse. What came out during the ceremony, held atop Mount Tam on a beautiful April day in 1977, was this, to which I gave the traditional-style name of

The Discourse on Freedom through Good Companionship.

Thus have I heard. On one occasion the Blessed One was staying in the Squirrels' Grove, among the trees, and in his company were five hundred monks and five hundred lay-people, five hundred Great Beings Mahāsattvas, five hundred Bodhisattvas from the ten quarters, and one thousand shining deities.

And the Blessed One saw the hearts and minds of all those in his company. And he addressed them, saying, O monks and lay-people, Mahāsattvas, Bodhisattvas, deities.

And they responded, Yes O Blessed One.

And the Blessed One said, The great ocean, O friends, has but one taste, that of salt. Just so is the Great Dharma, which has but one taste, that of freedom.

And what is the *path* to that freedom, O friends? The whole of the path to that freedom, O friends, consists totally in good companionship. To taste that freedom, O friends, walk always on the path of good companionship. Do not abandon good companionship in the hope of achieving freedom. In the Great Dharma there is no

18

conflict between these two. Indeed, it is only in the minds of the unseeing that there appears to be a conflict here.

And what is this good companionship, O friends? It is careful listening to one another, it is intimacy with one another, it is helpfulness to one another, O friends. And which careful listening, which intimacy, which helpfulness to one another are good companionship? Those that with seeing wisdom and with heartfelt compassion are conducive to the non-clinging freedom of the heart: *these* are good companionship.

Be of help, not of hindrance, O friends, to the going beyond clinging. Be of help to the going beyond fear. Be of help to the going beyond possessiveness. In this, develop the loving appreciation of one another. Indeed, this very appreciation, this love based solidly on mutual awareness, this seeing of each other's lived reality, are what lie beyond clinging. Know this as the path of good friendship, O friends!

And the hearts and the minds of those in the company of the Blessed One were gladdened, and they approved of the words of the Blessed One with one voice, saying, Wise and compassionate, indeed, are the words of the Blessed One.

And a great peace fell over that grove, where they all were gathered.

—Thus ends the discourse of the Blessed One entitled The Discourse on Freedom through Good Companionship (Kalyāṇamittatā-vimuttisutta).

YOUR ANGER

Your anger slashes through me, sabre-sharp.
I cry for the two of us.

Remembrance of warmth leads to hopes of a rebirth and a
rekindling of those now-gone, once-harmonized feelings. Here,
hope is a fish-hook in our heart!

I SEE NO LIMITS

I see no limits to this pain I feel.
This love is one with the hurt
                        pain
                        torment.
Sad is this growing separate
where once there was oneness.
I see you clearly
with love that breathes through all
            my body
I cannot remove you from
even one cell of my being.
Else, I am empty.
So many tears.
In the end, energies exhausted,
a reign of fatigue —
a calm soft quiet.
Blessèd be fatigue.
Gentle slow breaths.

ACTIVE PATIENCE
 the pain
 the looking away
 the slip into oblivion

 the dark pit
 the lost soul
 the helplessness

 the giving up
 the letting go

 the sense of clouds, of fog
 the sense of time
 the sense of limit

 the sense of end
 the sense of direction

 the will to look

 the joy of change

 the strength to look
 the sight of progress

 the energy to flow

 the harmony
 the nonresistance
 the welcoming

 the unlocking
 the floating
 the freedom.

MAKING WAR ON EGO

There is so much hostility! We may talk of "choiceless awareness," which is an attentiveness to experience that is non-judgmentally open to any and whatever mental-physical occurrence.

But despite this sort of talk, we still experience dis-pleasures, dis-satisfactions, frustrations.

Perhaps our awareness is keen at these moments. Experience may perceive patterns, in which these frustrations precede later attacks, criticisms, or angry outbursts (in bodily action or word, or in thought/imagination). As is said, frustration leads to aggression.

What happens may be noticed when the frustration-aggression involves us and others, or simply us and ourselves.

Our painful patterns may lead to a desire to have them end (a form of the thirst for extinction, vibhava-taṇhā, spoken of in Buddhist psychology). This sometimes takes the form of a resolution: "I won't criticize again." Or as a wish: "I wish these petty ego activities were fully stopped." Iconography represents this ego-stoppage by a large central figure holding down a tiny, struggling person by stepping on it firmly.

This is making war on ego. Besides being a manifestation of dualistic thinking, or alienated experience, it nurtures resistance to our process. Rather than learn from the situation, how we ("ego") are functioning, we reject the process and attempt to annihilate or at least fully suppress it.

A resolution often darkens our clarity of perception, so that we do not see the dissatisfying mechanics. When we cannot see in sufficient detail to dismantle the damaging contraption, we waste energy in our overkill activity: rather than loosening one screw, we try to pulverize steel! So we must be aware of the feeling of resolution that often accompanies the making of a resolution. This is blindness pretending to be perspicacity.

But seeing into the process is difficult when we are militant against it: "Hey! Are you still doing that horrible thing!"

Now, what kind of a response will *that* bring about? An open, caring curiosity and love about the "horrible" thing, or a self-defensive, strongly identifying with the thing as one's own action?

22

"Say! Now that's worth looking into more! That's important! It can be very freeing to understand how that works better, how each step of that process moves into the next!"

We can relate to frustrating patterns in ourselves and in others with either of these two attitudes.

Welcoming in these processes, as opportunities to see what was unseen, to understand what was not understood or was misunderstood, to be clearly aware of what was not in awareness — this welcoming frees our energies for the function of investigation rather than channeling them into suppressing these processes.

The Buddha did not attempt to kill Māra. He simply saw what Māra, the friend of the deadened, the death-like, was up to. He saw Māra's attempts to distract from awareness. And then Māra was powerless. All this without hostility: Hello, Māra! What are you doing now? Oh, I see.

And then Māra would go away.

Anyway, that's the Buddha and Māra.

With us, maybe we'll see our "ego" (giving a name but not especially an independent reality to various of our psychophysical processes), our desires for love, and security, and self-aggrandizement, and respect, in play (friendly or hostile) with another ego. If we are hostile to these processes of ourselves, we can see that hostility ooze over to the similar processes of the other. And vice-versa. This hostility may arise from earlier frustrations. When we can see all this, we're not tied into it: at first not so deeply; gradually, not at all.

When we see these processes occurring, we can learn compassion, be compassionate. This so-called ego is a needy thing, but it is ignorant about what it wants, and is destined to be frustrated (in part because of this ignorance). The ego is self-frustrating, like a drop of water which rests on the shore and longs to know the sea, not realizing that it is not held back from entering the sea. Poor ego! Can we give it love and our sympathy (but not condescending pity)? Or do we demand of processes we call ego, a non-egoic "enlightened" perspective? Isn't that a silly thing to expect from ego? Why, then, later attack it for not fulfilling our silly demands?

23

WE WANT NOT TO SEE

We want not to see what we take to be painful or ugly.
So we don't look.
From not looking comes not seeing.
From not seeing comes not knowing.
From not knowing comes lack of confidence.
From lack of confidence come brittleness, fragility, insecurity.
From brittleness and such comes fear.
From fear comes defensiveness.
From defensiveness comes hostility.
From hostility comes lack of understanding of others.
From lack of understanding comes lack of compassion.
From lack of compassion comes superficiality of relationship.
From superficiality of relationship comes frustration
    in the sphere of love.
From love frustration comes pain.

Not wanting to see pain or ugliness, we close ourselves in,
    creating some of the very pain
    we will later find ourselves
    experiencing or
    engaged in a further effort to avoid experiencing.

When we see that this is the price we pay for not looking,
    we are more willing to look even at what we take
    at first glance to be painful.

POSING DILEMMAS

We are in the middle of something. Some activity is ongoing. The question arises, "What should I do here?" We may see an urge to go on with what is happening and at the same time a contrary urge to cut it off: Should I keep on with this, or am I off course, off the Middle Path, and should I change course?

Here we are posing a dilemma to ourselves. Here we feel a deci–sion may be appropriate. Do we stick ourselves on one of the two horns of our dilemma and call that a decision, a solution? Let's not forget: There is no decision that has to be made. First, we either notice and appreciate that a dilemma is being posed, or, we do not. Then, we perhaps see that this is arising out of a conflict that we feel, no longer sure and content within ourselves about what is happening, about what we are doing, or, we do not.

If patience is allowing us to stay with this situation, if we do not attempt to "resolve" this situation by taking a stand on what ought to be done, then we will have the opportunity to see what our uneasiness is about, to see what is underlying those questions which arose a moment earlier.

Since there is some sort of conflict here, we will see more than one thing here: there will be here at least two unharmonious elements, such as interests, desires, concerns, and perhaps several or even many. And perhaps we will appreciate what is disturbing us on several levels-specific desires, general attitudes, even life plans of ours coming in here.

In this investigation (anupassanā) we have left behind looking at ourselves as simple, unified beings: "That bothers me because I am who I am."

Now, we see more clearly the various elements that make us up: What we see are particular desires, preferences, feelings, hopes, fears, images, thoughts, whatever.

Here we see, in Buddhist terms, the dharmas that we note, in sequence, when we practice mindfulness. We shift here to seeing these various discrete factors of consciousness, discrete yet clearly interrelated, inter-influencing. And now, whether we use the lan-guage of "I" and "mine" and "you" and "yours," or not, we are in a position to appreciate these various and distinct active tendencies within ourselves which are structuring our joys and sadnesses.

One function of the oft-repeated Zenny questions such as "Who is the 'I' who desires?" and "Who is the 'I' who sees?" and so forth, is to bring about this shift.

But perhaps we do see a decision coming up, and we feel that the issue has been resolved. The tension we felt while stuck between alternatives feels relieved. We can relax.

We know from experience that deciding after deliberating relaxes us. It definitely has an immediate calming effect. This effect may only last a moment before the nagging question arises of whether our decision was the proper one, but a short-lived effect is as real as an enduring one. Yet, here we remember that decisions only push our energies in one of the two or more directions involved, but do not eliminate the unharmonious elements which a moment before were all active in our minds (and bodies). In this way we see more clearly that disparate desires and so forth are not harmonized by a decision, but some merely redirected, some suppressed, some nurtured, etc.

The attitude of mindfulness is one of What is going on here? of What are the roots or sources of these vacillations and deliberations? and not one of What should I decide here?

NUTS

Why can't we eat just one salted nut and stop?

Well, we can.

If we stop after just one, we notice that the taste lingers on. This taste brings back to mind what we have just eaten. It has us be conscious of our recent mouth-centered gustatory experience. The taste fades slowly and various images and ideas and thoughts about it come and go. This experience is subtle; it is enough — if we allow it to evolve just as it is evolving.

This subtle experience can bring on a reaction in the mind. The mind often prefers strong experience to subtle experience, as when it, going dull on a monotonous ache, longs for sharp pain. It becomes impatient, as if being tickled too lightly.

Here we see the mind hesitating at letting our experience be and simply becoming more alert if what is happening is not "loud" enough. We see, instead, its tendency to intensify, to amplify the experience somehow.

This interferes with the process and its own natural speed (or slowness) and intensity (or blandness). Then, whether the process is that of the fading taste of a salted nut or of any occurrence in our life, we don't experience such a process according to its own rhythm, but, rather, according to how we feel most comfortable.

Then we frequently find the desire to have the process grow "louder" (if subtle, a tickling anxiety). Or, find the desire for it to have disappeared and ended already (if subtle, an annoyance anxiety). Either such desire tends to cut off our simply watching a process dissolve on its own, following its own nature.

Can we see how often we go in a karmic way here, in general?

EMPTINESS FOR THE DISTRACTED MIND

Sometimes we feel totally distracted. There's just no concentration. We are tossed all over the place, so that we are lost. We have lost ourselves.

This is almost right, almost correct. But we have a body, and so our energy is never totally scattered. We can't get totally spaced out.

The body is there (here) when we feel distracted. If we feel distracted, first we recognize the distracted mind. If we are lost we can look for ourselves. And if we can look we will always find ourselves; the body is something we always have with us. So we look and see: "Oh, here we are."

We can stay with the body when we feel a lack of concentration. Not in the way of blocking out from our awareness what might be distracting us, but as the center from which we experience. When sounds come to us, we hear them. We do not have to go out to them. We stay at our center, and let all of our experiences come through us. This center is nothing special, nothing particular. In itself it is nothing, only the possibility of experience, only the place of emptiness in which experiences can happen. We let sounds in. They can go in one ear and out the other. We do not try to hold them in our head. We simply notice them fully as they come through our center. Then when they are done, they are gone.

So we do not have to reach out for experience. We are fully open, letting in, and then out, all experience. We stay resting, fully in touch with the How, and totally without being swept away and drowned by it all. We are like the tortoise. It pulls in all its limbs, its head, its tail, reaching out to nothing. But it is not disconnected, dissociated from its environment. It is still in the context it's in. It still has contact. But it is not grabby; it does not lose stability by over-reaching. We allow ourselves body-awareness, we stay aware of our body, and we too stay undistracted, knowing where we are, what we feel, open to all experiences flowing through us.

MIND CLOUDS

When we sit in a quiet place and begin to notice the flow of consciousness, its initial noisiness becomes evident to us. Rather than experiencing calm tranquility, we see before us a mind like a butterfly. It darts unpredictably all over our field of consciousness, landing for an instant now here, now there, and then it's off again. If we try to catch hold of this butterfly-mind, it can become strongly elusive. Our reaching out for this darting-about mind can be frustrating, tiring, and discouraging. We feel we are having a bad meditation and then wonder if we will ever do the thing correctly. It didn't sound so difficult, after all, this simply being watchful!

At such times the noisiness of the mind may become drone-like, hypnotic. Awareness is out of focus. We feel ourselves in a psychological fog. We know the mind is not still, we know something is happening, but we cannot notice what it is. Experience may be very smooth and in a way even peaceful, like being enveloped in a cocoon or in a billowy cloud. We float along with little agitation. Perhaps it becomes so smooth that we hunch over or even tilt over. Our head may drop as we fall asleep; perhaps we catch ourselves snoring. (Snoring is a way we have of waking ourselves up.)

We realize we are floating along not noticing very clearly what is going through consciousness. Long memories or contemplations of some future situation or even sheer fantasies make up the contents of our daydreaming. And our later recollection of our daydreams is very selective. When we snap out of a daydream we can return to perhaps one or two scenes from the dream. That is often the limit of our awareness.

There are even times when we are totally oblivious to what is happening, even to the feeling that we are missing something. Obliviousness is totally forgetting an experience from the instant it occurs onwards. And when we are totally unaware of what is happening we are like the walking dead. Is death what we want from life?

If we are sitting with the intention of practicing mindfulness, and this is what our flow of consciousness is like, great discouragement and doubt may come up. When this happens we can use this initially "negative" energy, welcoming it. When we make no attempt to suppress this negative energy, we do not exhaust ourselves. Instead of resisting the doubt and the discouragement, we guide their flow by our attentiveness to them: *they* become polite guests, and *we* are not controlled by their "negativity." Instead they provide us with energy that we use in a way helpful to our meditation. So this doubt and discouragement can be changed from powerful enemies to useful allies: the Buddha likens our lack of clarity to a fire burning low. What is needed to bring this fire to a healthy state again is dry kindling wood, which is whatever helps by energizing the psychological process. Doubt and discouragement make excellent kindling wood!

We may first notice the old rut here of our criticizing ourselves, depressing ourselves with our ideas of what we conceive a good period of meditation to be. This rut may seem hard to get out of. But when we let go of the ideas of what good meditation is, and what bad meditation is, we can more easily get on with the meditating. Which is to say, get on with simply noticing whatever comes into awareness, its origin, its growth and development, and its deterioration and ending. We watch the full life of these objects of awareness, and then we understand them, that is, we understand ourselves.

So perhaps we are feeling that we are stuck in the cloud-like state of mind, and we begin experiencing discouragement and doubt. How do we treat this experience? We notice its presence. We see what the discouragement is, what the doubt is. We do this by investigating how each of these appears to us. Then we see that each such appearance is simply one more object for awareness.

The mind may suggest that we are stuck just too strongly here to get unstuck. The thought may occur to us that this sleep-like state of mind has its own on-rolling momentum, difficult to slow down or to stop. This thought is a theory or idea about what is and what isn't easy. We can fully acknowledge this idea, then see just how difficult it claims the task is, see just what this theory is claiming, and become skeptical but open-minded scientists in search of the truth.

We can see that energy is available from this self-discouraging and doubting. Of course *their* aim is to discourage and to keep us from carrying on in the practice. What else would we expect self-discouraging and doubting to be aimed towards? But there is no need to go where they lead. So we ask, "What are you up to now? What are you designed to discourage? What is to be doubted?"

It is important to look at this discouraging and doubting. We learn what has brought them about and see what they are to do, how they are supposed to function. And then they are powerless.

Or does it all still feel hopeless? Do you have the idea of giving it all up at such a point, concluding that there's nothing really to be gotten from something as silly as simply sitting, motionless? And you know it's not comfortable! Perhaps the thought comes, "I think I'll have a smoke or a drink, or some company, some loving, or read a book, dance, or listen to some music." And on and on.

So what is the reality here? There is surely quite a bit here to notice. Investigation now will be quite fruitful, energizing. And this is exactly what is needed for our fires that had burned down. So we look at just this point in time: Our awareness was still low, nothing was yet especially clear. So what was in our consciousness was out of focus. We couldn't quite make it out. This is the first thing there is for us to acknowledge.

Have you ever felt that you almost see something just before you again sink into one more period of obliviousness? We can shift now when such a feeling arises again into looking at the lack of focus. We look at how it's working.

When something is out of focus, what *is* happening? We can imagine focusing our vision at some point. If an object is not at this focal point, it will be out of focus. When in meditation things are out of focus, are *they* not at the focal point, not at the right place to be seen clearly? But how can they *not* be at the right place? After all, what we look at *here*, in meditation, is what is happening in consciousness, what is the present reality. And reality, after all, is *always* what it is, and not otherwise. Surely if we want to see the present reality itself, it is most simple to look at it directly, and not try to recreate it as our desires or imagination say it should be.

So we have something here influencing our gaze. Our gaze is not focused on what's happening. So why is what is happening out of focus? If we are looking out of focus, we can change our focus. Perhaps we have been trying to perceive an impressionist painting with an electron microscope. Surely we can put down the microscope. Now, how do we know how to look, where to look? This is no question. We do not have a problem here, only our desire to have it all set up for us beforehand with a money-back guarantee. But we're in the wrong showroom for that! Reality writes no guarantees.

So why *don't* we have a problem? Because we do not need to know where to look, how to look. We just look. We must give up the idea that we know where to look and then we will be able just to look: we see what is most easy to see. For that's what there is to look at. Simple! There was a simple rule, or instruction, expressed in the *Visuddhimagga* (*The Path of Purification*), by Buddhaghosa, from some 900 years after the time of the Buddha, or so I thought for years. Neither I nor any monk-scholars that I have consulted through the decades, though, can find any such statement there. So I am not sure where this simple rule was first stated. In any case, I can still suggest here that if mindfulness meditation has any rule, it's simply: *Notice whatever is most prominent in consciousness and continue on doing that.* That's all. If it's getting hard, just look again. Perhaps you will notice then that you are unnecessarily straining. Now, do you see what leads to that straining?

Perhaps in your desire to get out of this mental torpor you have focused on the breathing sensations. Then when this fails, you may remember that the Buddha looked at this, looked at concentrating when there is low awareness. And he compared it to someone's responding to a low fire trying to revive it by heaping on wet leaves.

So you may work at finely focusing the attention on the breath at the tip of the nose, or on the movements of the belly in breathing, until all awareness is overcome by sleepiness, all yawning is gone, and sound sleep takes over. If we are too finely focused we will be as good as blind. If our full body is all that we can barely perceive, can we accept that as the object of meditation? If not, we are blinding ourselves with a rule about what is or isn't an appropriate meditation object.

It is important to look at this preference for one meditation object over another whenever we come across this mental drowsiness, known in Buddhism as Sloth and Torpor, the Third Hindrance. Can we see what our preference in the given instance is? Something *is* arising in consciousness which we prefer *wouldn't* be. Or something is *not* arising in consciousness that we prefer *would* be. So we are separating ourselves from whatever the present reality is. We are separating ourselves from reality, keeping ourselves back, and this is known in Buddhism as dukkha, and known to all of us as living reluctantly through a dissatisfying experience.

Can we see this dissatisfaction clearly? Can we look into what preferences are alive here? Can we see these preferences bringing about our resistance to what is happening, to the present stage of ever-changing reality? Why are we working so hard to make difficulties for ourselves? We can see, each of us, what in this and what in that context is disturbing to us, what we do to resist, and what brings on this resisting. When we see the harm we do to ourselves out of ignorance and lack of skill in our activities, we learn skillfulness, practical wisdom. Then there can be an end of these activities that we found harmful. The way out of the pain of carrying something burdensome is to lay down the burden. It is the stopping of *all* such practices that we call nirvāṇa. But what follows is not the end of *everything*; what follows is simply the end of the pain those practices entail.

There is in every unclear mind some preference for reality to be other than it is. What do we want not to be happening? If we ask ourselves this question, and then do *not* attempt to figure out the answer, but rather simply let come whatever comes to mind, we will be approached by the answer. All that is helpful for us is to be waiting patiently and attentively.

But perhaps when we pose this question, and let the answer come, it will be painful for us. It might even be the very dissatisfaction that is at the root of our present unclear, foggy, or wandering mind. So! Is this in turn just an idea, a premonition, a fear we use to keep from seeing the reality that we enslave ourselves by? Let us see this idea, this fear, but still look to see what comes to us: we look at the reality long enough to see our reactions, to learn which biases and inclinations there are still alive in us. Slowly we become free of them through this seeing. *This path to freedom is a gradual path.* When we pose this question about our preferences, do we pain-fully glimpse that root dissatisfaction once again? *Did* we get a glimpse of it once again just then? Is it back in all its original painfulness? Does this reopen an old wound? *Do* we have a painful old wound here? If so, we can see now that this wound that still pains us has never been properly cared for. Here is our chance. Now we can finally treat our wounds successfully. So what is there for us doctors to do? When we were little children we used to play doctor. All we had to do then was to bandage imagined cuts over. We do not have to limit our helpful procedures *now* to what we then played around with. Our insight has certainly grown since *then*! We must learn now how to help our wounds heal. We can be grateful that these wounds of ours are so patient that they will reopen for us over and over while we try different treatments, until we learn how to heal! Why chase away, then, our best teachers? We look now. We carefully examine what needs treatment, and then we *see* the treatment that is appropriate. Or do we really think, even now, that, no matter what the wound, a big enough bandaging will not only *cover* but also actually *heal* it?

So it is time to look. We look here without knowing what we will see. Our *thought* that we have mental drowsiness, and our dissatisfaction about this drowsiness could combine to convince us that we know our state of mind. But this I-know-how-I'm-feeling attitude will blind us to clarity of awareness as it emerges. So *we keep a check that this attitude does not take control.* Then we may notice, "O, everything is quite clear again!" Or perhaps what is most striking in our consciousness is the intensity of the reopened wound, the present dissatisfaction. Pain whether physical or psychological has the capacity to bring about impressive clarity!

We take time to note well this present dissatisfaction. No one said that it would be comfortable for us to look at what is making us uncomfortable. It is uncomfortable for us either way. Yet, if we bring deep attentiveness with us we can let go of everything else, everything painful, and so get through the troubled waters we occasionally meet in life's journeying. Do we have the patience and the courage to help ourselves through these? With mindfulness, the waters we go across are more invigorating and enjoyable than we sometimes suppose them to be.

There is true living waiting for us if we are continually watchful: with this mindfulness we can end our death-like state and fully *live* through life's journeying. We call this, voyaging over to the far shore.

THE DESIRE FOR FREEDOM

Life brings with it not only pleasures but also pains. We can see this, and when this is clear to us, when we have no doubt about this, we may see a desire arise to be free of this pain. This is a desire for freedom.

We can want freedom. We can see how this desire for freedom works and also, maybe, how it is kept from working.

Sometimes we take on a theory about desires and how they are *all* undesirable, how *any* desire is tied in with pain, and so it doesn't matter what the particular desire is; any desire is a desire and (therefore, for that fact alone) to be avoided.

This idea can lead us to fight the desire for freedom, to resist it. If we *look* at desires, we can see that every desire is a desire. We can also see that certain desires lead in one direction, and other desires lead in another direction. There's a difference here between different desires, even if they are all alike in one way. There is the special desire, to end all desires. If we cut against that desire, if we suppress that desire and its force, there is perhaps not the energy to break away from the systems we are locked into, from the conditioning that we are.

We have a conditioned aspect to ourselves. This wants freedom, too, Freedom sounds nice. "Yes, I would like to be free." Attracted toward this freedom, we think, "Oh, I'm going to a two-week meditation retreat. I hope I'll leave it enlightened. *That's* all I really want!"

This desire for freedom is coming from conditioning. We can see here how conditioning imagines freedom to be: a state in which the conditioning has its own way, where the desires coming out of conditioning run rampant, unrestrictedly. That's called freedom of the self, freedom of the ego. This is like being released from prison: the end of external constraints on self-fulfillment.

Freedom *of* the self is freedom for conditioning to form deeper and deeper ruts, working towards its preconception of what will satisfy.

Freedom of another sort is freedom *from* the self, freedom from the ego, from the conditioned mind, freedom from conditioning.

Out of this very conditioning, out of this conditioned mind, comes an "understanding" of freedom that is a limited understanding. It must be limited: like a fish which has no experience of the dry land, no basis for knowing what is beyond the lake it knows as its world. Its limit is its lake; its lake is its conditioning.

Still, conditioned mind tries to go beyond the conditioning and even wants to be that which goes beyond the conditioning. But of course conditioned mind, the conditioning, cannot itself go beyond conditioning.

We simply let this conditioning be, as limited as it is. We do not stay in its confined world by arguing with it, or fighting it. To go outside we don't destroy the building we're in; we just go outside. And where is this outside? It is not literally somewhere else!

In moving along the path to freedom, we do not have to direct ourselves in any given direction, or go anywhere at all! In fact, when we notice a channeling of the flow of life, we can see the work of our preconceptions, of our limited desires, of one or another aspect of our conditioning. There is nothing "wrong" or "bad" about this. But we are not deluded into thinking that this is something it isn't. It isn't seeing into conditioning and its manifestation; it *is* that conditioning and manifestation. All there is to do is to appreciate how this conditioning can work at very subtle or very sublime levels. We know that when this is not clearly appreciated, there is often a tendency for pride to arise, a possessiveness about what is imagined to be a very "high" state! This is just one more form of creating a self-image.

We can watch here how our preconceptions, or, to use a word, how the "ego" tries to regulate the flow of life. We watch how it doesn't know where to go, but thinks that it knows. We can watch how it usually steers away from pain.

We can see how strong this tendency to avoid pain is in us; it's a very strong tendency. It's much easier, or, rather, sometimes it *feels* much easier, to get into loving and joyful feelings. It's very difficult then to feel the negativity that's there. This doesn't mean that there is no negativity there, but that our experience is bent over toward the pleasant. We can go around then talking about loving feelings, about how good we feel about everything and everyone: maybe we wear a tee-shirt with the words over our chest, "Love everyone." We can go around doing those sorts of things if we want.

But the first thing is to experience: then the talk will follow the experience.

We can see a preference, thinking that the way out of something unpleasant is by steering out of it. When we clearly see the process of avoidance, attentiveness is present; the not looking at a "problem" is looked at. Looking has moved in where there was avoidance of looking! Going *around* our present situation becomes a going *through* it! Then we can go through to the other side; not getting stuck in the unpleasantness, but not avoiding it, either.

This is going on beyond conditioning, not by avoiding conditioning, but by going through conditioning.

We let what is happening in our present life show itself to us. This going through conditioning has a very simple aspect: it takes no plan. No plan of ego is required, no plan of ego is appropriate to end ego. Ego is not going to do that. While ego is operating, its own effort, its own tendency, is towards strengthening its own pattern, however it accomplishes that. Perhaps it uses fear: "Yes, here's a danger. I'd better stay out of this situation. I can't take this at all!" If we listen to such a train of thoughts, we strengthen our conditioning. That's the way fear works, to stay with that example here.

Going beyond conditioning does not take fighting conditioning. We simply see here that conditioning isn't the whole picture, the whole reality. We see that conditioning will tend to maintain itself, to keep things as comfortable as possible, stable, within its own limits.

While we are watching conditioning, we have an opportunity to look into ourselves, into our pains. We do not merely see that something involves pain for us: indeed, *if we see only that there is pain, we do not see the full reality*. We can also see the specific things that are bothersome to us, how they work, how they bother us, how we are bothered.

When we start out as the fish, all that we see are the specifics of our conditioned existence. In the process of watching these specifics of our conditioned existence, we naturally come to see the limits, the edges, the borders, the boundaries of this conditioned existence. Through the experience of the conditioned comes the appreciation of the non-conditioned. This appreciation is the space in which the conditioned can be, in which it can be easily allowed to be. This space is like an island which is unbothered by waves beating against the shore, like a cool spot under a shade tree which is not overheated by a broiling sun. It is a way of experience that *allows* conditioning, without putting energy into that conditioning. So the conditioning has only *its* old momentum, but no new energy. With patience we can see its momentum diminish, like a once-roaring fire that has not been fed new branches and is now only embers.

This process of letting painful conditioned patterns roll down to a stop, or burn out, involves our patience. And, with our continual attention, there is little, if any, energy feeding the conditioning processes now on the wane. Still, this is not a picnic.

Or maybe it is. If we can have a picnic, or not have a picnic, we are free to have a picnic when life is a picnic for us, and free not to, when it isn't.

VIPASSANĀ SHMIPASSANĀ

It may dawn on you that vipassanā isn't so great. That it is a waste of time. That there is no value in formal sitting practice, nor in there being a meditation center. At least, definitely not in a way personally involving you. Then we can hear ourselves ask the question of "Why do any more sitting?" or "Why stay at the meditation center any longer?" This may lead to conclusions — thoughts or images about starting some other activity: standing up, or travelling away from the center. We may see ourselves decide to drop out of the vipassanā scene altogether. What was this vipassanā supposed to do, anyway? Did it once actually have some appeal?

Do we feel ashamed to ask such questions, or defiant? Such questions may strike us as heretical. Or as disrespectful. Or, put a Buddhist way, as a manifestation of Ignorance. So we may put these questions aside as worthless or bad in some sense. We see that feelings can be suppressed this way. Done in the lofty name of Buddhism, perhaps, but still a way of suppression.

Can't we just transcend Buddhist concepts for a minute, and accept how we feel?

Let's allow questioning. Questioning irritates the dogmatic mind and frustrates the desire for certainty. Questioning clears out mental drowsiness. It energizes our alertness. It leads to deep insight. The greater the doubt, as some put it, the greater the satori.

In the questioning mind is the natural tendency to investigate our present situation. This is the way of discovery through the presence of mindfulness on a practical level.

When we see this questioning, what is it, really, that is being questioned? There is some image or concept of a practice here, and a dissatisfaction with that practice: it isn't producing what we wanted! "Hey! I've been 'doing vipassanā' for almost a decade now, and I still (fill in your own rut here)!"

Disappointed expectations. Impatience. Troublesome times. Something in our trip through human existence we aren't content about.

Are we fighting our situation? Well, what is our situation? Do we identify our dissatisfaction as "vipassanā"! ? Come on now, really!! Are we angry at an idea (!) for our continuing life, an all-too-human existence? Imagine that! Did we really think, imagine, that life would stop going through its changes, its challenges, just because we sit still a few hours a day or live in a community of "spiritually"-oriented friends, perhaps among "high" and "developed" individuals? This imagination of ours is supplying us here with distractions and scapegoats to defuse later frustrations, isn't it?

In any case, here we still are. Even the Buddha grew old and died. Life hasn't stopped going through its changes here either. Will our imagination lead us to focus our dissatisfaction here on a sitting practice, or on the quality of a community, or on those individuals who *must* be, after all, not really so high and developed?

This sees the animation of our own life processes as coming from outside, over there somewhere. When we are this way and we notice joy, happiness, loving feelings, we may feel gratitude for the Teaching. Or for the teacher. And when we notice misery, dejection, hate, we may feel resentful against the limits of this, after all, not so wonderful Teaching. Or against the limits of the teacher! This is like breaking a mirror for what we see in it.

It doesn't matter if we follow this mirror-breaking way of dealing with our situation or not. It doesn't matter if we stop the practice of sitting meditation, if we leave a meditation center. (This is *not* to say that it makes no difference.) In either case, we have ourselves with us. In either case, life goes on. In either case, life's concerns are still there for us to deal with.

Check it out for yourself. Isn't it so? And *if* so, where do *you* go from here!

DO WHAT TEACHES

Do what teaches.
Leave behind what reteaches what you already know.
Watch energy born of fear, worried energy, energy for keeping us in
        place, for locking out the unknown.
Dive into the void.

Learning to face what is difficult, we come to see what brings along
something strikingly unpleasant, painful, with it.

We see what the whole situation calls for, rather than focusing on
        what we happen to want at the moment.

We travel through all sorts of spaces, experiences, situations, using
        whatever comes along to grow from, to learn through, to
        appreciate. Then it doesn't matter much what it is specifi-
        cally that comes along. We become a chameleon that lets
        itself be fully absorbed into each experience, in symphony
        with each new situation, and yet the chameleon goes on.
        There is this resonating, this sympathizing, in experience
        more and more deeply.

RECOLLECTIONS

Recollections of
        the you you were and the way they saw you,
        the beliefs you held,
        the feelings you felt.
Just recollections.
You don't know yourself anymore —
live and learn.
                        Open-eyed, just seeing what is,
                        grounded in awareness,
                        grounded anywhere,
                        grounded everywhere.
Groundless traveler always at home.

WHERE'S THE LOVE IN VIPASSANĀ?

Q: Vipassanā Meditation seems one-sided to me, lacking in love. How does love, the heart, come into Vipassanā practice? *I* can't see it!

A: Yes, how does the heart come into Vipassanā? You may feel that Vipassanā is dry and cold. Or that may be your experience now in meditation: the heavy sense that there are no feelings of love in the present moment. And under all of that, there is a valuing of the Way of the Heart. We can look and see if we have an image of Vipassanā here, containing in it a desire or a demand for it to be something specific, or to do something specific for us.

We can understand that Vipassanā Meditation is not a particular feeling or emotion or psychological state or physical state. It is no particular experience at all. It has no given form. It is just a space in which we have the possibility of seeing whatever it is that comes to us in life.

This space we call "Vipassanā" may allow us to see love, if we are feeling love. It may allow us to see the limit of love, if the love we are aware of has a limit. The space itself is neither the fullness, nor the limit, of love. We can appreciate that here.

What is central here is the valuing of the Way of the Heart, the Way of Caring, which underlies this uneasiness about Vipassanā practice. Yet we can see that this empty space of mindfulness is bringing you more deeply in touch with your own compassionate nature.

Can you see it now?

GROWTH THROUGH LOVE

Love can make us grow. Do we have this type of love between us and those we love? Do we relate in a way that allows for expansion and growth in depth — for the other we feel we love, and for ourselves?

We sometimes relate in a critical, unaccepting way. We want something from the other person that is not forthcoming. This can lead to a feeling of hurt or rejection that can in turn lead to a defensive withdrawal or to a defensive attacking. Then the other often responds by not accepting *our* unaccepting stance.

But we can each go on now to simply seeing what the other is experiencing and how the other is changing. We have no need to withdraw or to attack when we see fully and acknowledge *deeply*, first of all to ourselves, and then to the other, what we see. This is *called* being accepting. It is simply the perception of what is happening, and allowing it to resonate for us, in us.

Then we can gently guide ourselves, and one another, to a more accepting, expansive, courageous, more welcoming frame of mind.

SPIRITUAL RELATIONSHIP

What makes a relationship spiritual, we might guess, is that in it we are relating to something spiritual, something divine, godly, or other-worldly. I want to suggest, rather, that in it we are relating to something spiritually. It is a matter of how we relate, rather than of *what* we relate to. It is a matter of attitude.

This attitude allows us to relate as an ally in the exploration of life. How do we become allies with those we relate to? By coming to the other aware that we are fellow travellers, experiencing together the on-flowing show, and by our treating both of us as centers of life: with caring and open curiosity and wonderment. As allies, present, sharing and exchanging feelings, observations, reactions, and experiences in general. This caring curiosity of a comrade lives out the "spiritual" attitude; this attitude is a loving one, *one which leads to confident trust and openness*. This attitude allows an evolution, a growth, an expansion — one possible *in the context of* this relationship with another person, and *growing out of* this context: this context is love in this sense.

This love is deep heart-felt friendship-in-action. It is not a passively felt sensation, a twitching or an ache, not a passively held doctrine or credo, but an attitude in practice: it is an attitude that is carried into action, an attitude with ongoing manifestations. Love is having the belovèd's well being at heart. When this is based on an appreciation of what is happening for the belovèd, and is free from conflicting needs or demands of our own egos, this love can operate for the benefit of the belovèd. Love is flexible, being open to and responsive to the needs and yearnings of the belovèd. Love is not stubborn, rigid, or prideful; it is miraculous: The more we give love, the more love we have. For in giving love, as in making (creating) love, we experience love, and the more we experience love, the better we know it, the more its vitality glows through all our body. Loving the belovèd, giving our love to the belovèd, acting for the belovèd, rejuvenates the lover as much as it satisfies the belovèd. It enrichens both. It is what makes us rich human beings.*

* See more in Chapter 1 ("The Concept of Love and its Logic") of M. Ginsberg, *Calm, Clear, and Loving: Soothing the Distressed Mind, Healing the Wounded Heart* (Second edition, 2012), pp. 1-25.

SHIVA FRIENDSHIP

I shall play the wind, to your butterfly. Let me lift you to the sky; your flips and turns and rolls and drops let me guide. Invisible to all the others, you will feel my presence, embracing your every move through space.

I shall play the star, to your star. Let me twinkle back to you as we shine on. Light-years apart, we will be visible to one another, even when clouds darken the skies to all the others.

I shall play the non-intruder, to your lover. Let me feel your developing love for one another, know the growing intensity between you two, remain apart while you go where you know not.

I shall play the ineffable, to your silence. Beyond all words, beyond om, beyond, I shall abide in quiet. Waves let us accept, moving through us, neither ignored nor disturbing.

CUTTING SOME SLACK
(PRACTICAL CARING COMPASSION)

We may notice that at times we come to a clearer understanding of some issue that we facing, with a stronger sense of knowing what is important in it, and with a well-defined idea of how to act in order to deal wisely with the situation.

When this happens, we may notice a certainly we now feel that is beyond the situation and that becomes more like a dogmatic, unquestioning attitude than a wise perspective that will allow for the skillful application of thought, word, and action to the situation.

We may similarly find ourselves definite in our sense that we know the right way, and, relatedly, that we can see when we are not living in according with that (not "living up to" that standard) and see when others, too, are failing in similar ways. We may become rather judgmental in how we look at and experience what we and others are doing in order to try to live through the given situation with minimal harm and pain (for ourselves, for others, or for both).

This is a tendency of the perfectionist mind, where a clear idea of what to think, say, and do is confidently held, and where anything that we or others do that does not conform to that idea, we see as problematic, if not bad, if not (in a more extreme way of thinking about things) evil!

We may appear to others as self-righteous or condescending. We may see others as inferior or failing at this or that life task. We may let them know, either indirectly, softly, articulately, strongly, or even harshly. ("You just don't know how to take care of yourself!" "You are so insensitive!" "You really embarrassed me when we were at dinner with the McAdam family yesterday!" and so on.)

And, perhaps without speaking it out loud, we may have similar criticisms of ourselves. ("Why can't I be nicer to her when she is feeling down or overwhelmed?" "Why did I tell that person on the train that I was tired of hearing his blather?" and so on.)

We can perhaps easily imagine or remember even more harsh or otherwise unacceptable words or actions that we ourselves, or others, have taken, and that we had very strong judgments about, whether expressed to them or kept to ourselves.

What is this criticalness about? Why does it strike us (or many others, perhaps) as a bit of nastiness, or rigidity, or closed-mindedness? And what in our experience has the tendency to soften that and to make us more tolerant or gentle, more forgiving and less condescending, toward others and perhaps even toward ourselves?

Part of what is there to be seen, in any such problematic situation, is the dukkha or distress that we or others are feeling, and to notice how that influences what we and others then think, say, or do. This is not necessarily a matter of excusing anything, but of seeing into the ways in which people experience and deal with their worlds.

When we can see the underlying pain or discomfort that is alive and operating in given situations, a natural response to this is our native compassion when we see something untoward or unhappy going on. To avoid feeling this sympathic sadness and the natural wish that it be gone, finished, we must turn away or begin to criticize ("It's all your own fault" "Don't bother me with your problems!" "I have my own worries!" and so on.)

If we do not turn a cold heart on the situation, we may easily be touched by the sadness we are noticing. This in turn naturally brings an appreciation of the difficulties of life, not only in the given particular situation, but in general.

We may come to realize, especially in situations where we are with those we care about and who care about us, people that we have an ongoing or even long-term relationship with, that we all, individually and as a group (of two or more) want happiness and satisfaction in the relationship. We may not be skillful and elegant in doing what we are doing, or in saying what we are saying, but we often approximate, get close to, doing things well — *almost!*

Here there may be one or two things said or done that put things out of balance, or that raise the defensiveness of one of us, perhaps from the tone of voice being used, in the issues that are touched upon that are very sensitive (sore, raw) to the person becoming defensive. Here, and perhaps especially here, there is the opportunity to recognize that while trying to have an agreeable time, something else is happening as well, which is unpleasant or turbulent for at least one person involved.

We can become critical here, but we can also realize that while we are perhaps trying to do well, we are coming close but missing the target in some minor or minimal but perhaps very disturbing way.

Or, we can acknowledge that we are trying and that while we did not quite succeed with elegance and grace, we could try again.

If we make this explicit, we begin (or continue) operating with an awareness that can be shared, inviting all involved to look at the interaction with a bit of distance, to be able to see the process and to be more free to re-evaluate what has been going on, to be more free to modify our thoughts, words, and actions in more skillful ways.

With this we can cultivate a sympathetic compassion and caring appreciation of ourselves and others, the gentle understanding of the difficulties, challenges, limitations, and even torments we all live through, trying to deal in our limited ways with our life situations, without our desire for perfection distorting a recognition that good enough may be better than perfection (in short, "cutting some slack" for ourselves and for others, as some say).

FORGIVING AND RECOGNIZING NEW HORIZONS

We have perhaps often heard that we should forgive and forget, or at least that we should forgive, so that we stop being "stuck" in the past and "move on" to the present and the future.

Yet often what this process of forgiving amounts to, or how it is done, may make little or no sense. Or come across to us as being totally unrealistic and unattainable. And of course, we may have no desire to suggest that we feel that was done is totally acceptable and OK in all ways.

Some texts* have attempted to put this sort of issue into the life contexts that gave birth to the issue, in the first place. Here, we may address the question in a practical way, considering what has the power to shift our relationship with the events we are asked to forgive in ways that are liberating to us, whether or not this focuses on forgiving and whether or not this actually involves forgiving at all!

One thing seems clear and that is that this takes a shift in our understanding of what went on and its import or significance in our lives. Whether we focus on the past specific actions or events that would be the subject of forgiveness (or not), the central issue is one we may come to appreciate as involving a rethinking or a new understanding of these and their significance in our overall lives.

We may not know how to develop such a new understanding of the events in question, but we may remember that often, a problem that is considered in a given context, with given considerations that define the situation, may remain a problem within that context. What may be needed is a changing of context, meaning an enlarging of the considerations taken into account.

After all, often when we are incapable of deciding something, or cannot resolve some dilemma we are facing, or are confused by something that does not make very good sense, or any sense at all, for that matter, the reason is that we not have some relevant information that will allow for a decision, for a resolution of the dilemma, or clarity about what has been going on!

* For example, Chapter 18 ("Forgive and Remember") of M. Ginsberg, *Calm, Clear, and Loving: Soothing the Distressed Mind, Healing the Wounded Heart* (Second edition, 2012), pp. 247-257.

Here, the further relevant information, or considerations about the event we are contemplating forgiving, would be some considerations about our overall life in relation to that event.

Looking at our lives here in a more inclusive way, what we can come to see is some of the differences brought about by having lived through the event in question. This is not necessarily, not especially, what the event itself was about, what its point was, what the motivation or aim (innocent, unskillful, malicious, etc.) might have been, but what actually has happened in our lives that we can see as having been made possible because of the event (that we being asked to forgive or are considering whether to forgive or not).

For example, perhaps in a work situation we were put in the position of taking responsibility for some calamity (in which we might or might not have had a significant role, or any role at all), and because of which we might have quit or been fired.

That would be an immediate consequence, and we might not be happy with that at all, and look for someone or some group to blame.

In the larger scheme of things, though, what else might have come about because of being made the scapegoat of that work problem?

We might have begun searching for new work, for example, and perhaps even decided to try a different kind of work. We may have gone back to earlier dreams that were too "impractical" and carried them out. Or we may have stumbled, it would seem to us, on some new opportunity that we were now open to. And this may have opened up doors to some very satisfying activities, meeting people that were much more agreeable to spend time with, and so on.

This is, of course, just an imaginary elaboration of an imaginary example of something we might be tormented about and asked to be forgiving about. But it does illustrate that if we take a larger frame of activity (consider more activities or parts of our lives) and take a larger frame of time (considering more than just the days or weeks or even months following the problematic incidents), we may come to see what has come about in our lives that was ultimately made possible, even if not intentionally at all, by the events we have been asked to forgive.

This is transforming our relationship with a problematic past not by denying it or by pretending that we are neutral to the actions that we felt hurt or injured by, but by seeing what has come to us that we are happy about and can be thankful about. All of this cannot be done in an artificial or mechanical way, but if done in a way that allows us a true appreciation of something in our lives related historically, even if in convoluted ways, to the unfortunate events of the past, we can counterbalance the bitterness of that past with the sweet happiness of the benefits we have since come to pass.

TROUBLES IN RELATIONSHIP

At times we are alone. That's when we see how we feel in aloneness. If we live fully in aloneness, even if we have experiences of loneliness, we are not needy. When we live through aloneness, and deeply appreciate how this affects us, we enter into relationship without a compulsive neediness. Then we can let relationship be.

Relationship involves relating with others, being related to others, being in relation to them, letting them come into us, into our world, and allowing ourselves to enter theirs.

We may find that we enter into relation with another individual through some idea of relationship. For example, some people seem to be in love with being in love. I want to love someone, they say. Then relating which does occur is under the pressure of how they conceive of a loving form of relationship.

We may have ideas about what relating amounts to, or have a special idea about what a particular relationship is. This can confine our awareness of the other to the small world defined by that concept of relationship: for example, a man calls his life-mate and the mother of his child, Mama. Literally, this would make him her son. This may influence much of his awareness of this other person.

In this case, we are experiencing through the focused vision of concepts: a sister is just a sister, and not, for example, a person saddened because of some disturbing news. Here our understanding of relationship may blind us: we are bored when something important it happening, if we are not well aware of it.

Sometimes this relating through our idea can be exciting: this is my lover. This is my long-lost brother. This is my dying granddad. This is my newborn daughter. This excitement is one more form of Māyā. It keeps us, or can keep us, in the world of image, of social fictions, *overlooking the reality that is not captured by our thinking*. Trying to experience reality through our thinking is like trying to scratch the bottom of our foot through the shoe.

So even when we give ourselves excitement by thinking of what is happening in our relating with another in some specific way, we can be aware that we may be led by this way of thinking to come to be out of touch with something important. And when we are aware of this tendency, *then how we think of our relationship does not need to delimit what we can be aware of.*

When we are simply open to what there is going on, without these ideas closing in our experience, there is a fullness to the moment that is extremely rich, gently poignant, deeply alive. Is it really odd or paradoxical that relating this way, fully, with another human being, without defining that person as having this or that relation to us, can be so deep — even deeper than relating through a concept as seemingly vitalizing as My Darling Lover?

Our thinking about relationship may lead us to set up certain ideals, with which we compare every person we come into contact with. Our idea of a Good Relationship may make extra difficulties for us when we come into conflict, either subtle or gross, with someone we are relating to: "We have never had a fight in the fifty-five years we've been married," she said with contentment and pride. Is this good news? Bad news? Perhaps conflicts between the two were regularly suppressed. Perhaps not.

When conflicts arise in relationship, how are they dealt with? Or do we think that relationships should be without conflict? That they-will be, perhaps if the people involved are "harmoniously matched" at least, all milk and honey? Aside from the fact that a diet of only milk and honey might bring on nausea and diarrhea, if it could be had, this ideal defined by lack of turbulence may lead to ill feelings, to ill will, if and when turbulences do arrive.

So conflicts may be denied, or avoided: "if that's the way you feel, I'll just spend the night playing cards with the boys."

This may "work" for the short term, in that tension may be somewhat lessened when the next day rolls around. We have to see if this is how we want to go through life, never *relating* about the conflicts in relationship. Are these conflicts, part of the very juice of relationship, being treated as an annoying interference with the "real" stuff of it all?

In relationships these conflicts give us the opportunity to appreciate what is difficult for us, and for others. This way leads to greater contact rather than to a cutting off from the other or others involved. We can see our humanity this way. (We are all human beings.) (Or isn't that O.K.?)

We notice that these conflicts are dealt with, are responded to, in various different ways: sometimes with great reactivity, or with very little awareness of how each person involved understands what is happening, or how each person is feeling about and evaluating what is happening, or how each is lost or perhaps individually sees where or how to go on from the present turbulence.

We may appreciate that we are working through some pattern of reactivity, can see into some compulsiveness that has been driving us, can notice our great, hostile reactivity to some conflict, or notice that we are bypassing some fear and being closed-off.

If we are getting slapped around each time a conflict arises, we are dealing with a harsh interpersonal, social (inter-psychological) reality. We can see that some people are handling their frustrations this way. Do we feel that being fully aware of this when it occurs will lead us to end this relation? Or will lead us in compassion to going more deeply into the frustrations these attacks involve?

This isn't a matter of one way being the right way and some other way being wrong. The real value in relationships, in the particular, different forms of relationship that each of us is involved in at any given time, may have nothing to do with our ideas defining what relationships are about. Our ideas don't know. Reality isn't controlled by our ideas or beliefs, by our hopes or even our fears.

If there is pain or torment in this relationship, we see how it feels. If we see our energies going into continuing such a painful system, we see how this occurs, what moves our energies in this direction. If our energies are not "feeding" the process, we see how this system is either continuing from other energies, or ending on its own. In this way we see into our own contribution to relationships we are in and how they operate. We see into what we ourselves are like. We see what we like and engage ourselves in.

We may be afraid of noticing some undesirable traits here: "I'm mean, or inconsiderate, or selfish, or masochistic." This is identifying with processes that do not feel enriching to us. If we simply see how things are working, we will know. *When we know ourselves, we do not know any one, essential thing.* We simply appreciate how various modes of humanity occur, and whether they are constricting and poisonous, or expansive and nourishing.

LIBERATING RELATIONSHIP, SPIRITUAL LOVE, PĀRASAMGATE

Have you been involved in relationship these days, or recently? Maybe you've noticed you already have a well-defined idea of what a good relationship is — whether one that's healthy, or alive, or stimulating, satisfying, or expanding, or is it a peaceful one, or one that's fun, therapeutic, or exciting? And maybe you've noticed you also already have an idea of a bad one — whether that's a sick relationship, or a neurotic one, or one that's deadening and stagnating, peaceful and soporific, or a fun-and-games superficial one, a therapeutic, overworked one, or an exciting and agitating, upsetting one.

Whatever ideas we may have, we can look beyond our ideas in order to see what is actually happening for us in our relationships with others. To start with, we may notice that sometimes we feel a pull to a certain relationship, to a certain other person. They catch our attention and appeal to us. And whether we take the relationship to be good or bad, healthy or neurotic, reasonable or incomprehensible, workable or impossible, these certain relations just seem to light up our lives: they just click for us; sometimes *in spite of ourselves* and what we think we want or are looking for. Haven't you ever had this experience?

If we notice this, we can see in operation the fact that *relationships, as it were, choose us*. At least the undeniably powerful ones seem to do so. They are the ones we can't resist: what they hold for us is too deeply significant for us to deny them or to let them go by. This means that they are alive for us, that there are certain issues in us that they are relevant to. As some people say, they push our buttons, they give us a buzz, they talk our language, they turn us on.

In this sort of relationship that arises naturally and effortlessly, in a way that feels spontaneous and powerfully alive, we can learn a lot about ourselves; not about our *images* of ourselves, but about ourselves. In relationship we can see how we act, and what our efforts are concentrated on bringing us.

What we are bringing on ourselves in our overall way of being and acting in a relation may of course be strikingly different from what we earnestly think we want in a relationship. This in a way is an astonishing fact. And may be the source of a lot of pain. Isn't that so? I'm not saying this to lay down a criticism, or to suggest how we ought to be in relationship (whatever that way might be), but simply to acknowledge this complication explicitly.

And if there is a source of pain, there is pain. We may not look at what we are driving towards in relation and we may then experience not only surprise but also pain. If in this case we direct ourselves into an attack on ourselves or the other as masochistic, we may overlook just how this pain came about. The first thing is to appreciate what's happening. Name-calling doesn't help us to do this.

What we are actually involved in in our relationships may not be obvious to us at first, neither what we are working towards there nor what our deepest frustrations are there. It may take many similar relationships over decades for us to see these processes clearly.

And we are not working on only one level. So there are a number of these processes, whether satisfying or frustrating to us, to learn about. These are all extremely important lessons for us to learn about ourselves. What I mean about the difference between what we think we want and are doing in relationship on one hand, and what we are actually moving towards, on the other, may be made clearer by an example.

Terry and Pat meet each other. There is an attraction. They begin to spend time together, and so a relationship is born. After a while, the two begin to consider the possibility of living together; they begin experiencing one another as possible living partners. They feel that their relationship is in the air, on the balance, waiting for their decision. This is how they experience their time together.

Terry thinks that this time together is to allow the two to feel out what being with the other is like, and to allow each to see the other in a more natural, less put-on, less role-playing way. This is for Terry the whole point of the relation here. And Pat thinks that this time together is to enjoy things together, and go out together, and live in a social world where the two are related to by *other* people as a couple. This is for Pat the whole point of the relation here.

Now an interesting way I have come across to look at the ongoing reality of relationships is to ask this question: given how each is vis-à-vis the other, if this relation had been designed to teach each partner some definite life lesson, what would each's lesson be?

In this example, an outsider may be able to answer this question about the relationship between Terry and Pat with no hesitation or doubt, but the question may be totally mysterious for Terry or Pat.

For instance, it may be painfully obvious to friends and others but not to either Terry or Pat, that the great flow of Terry's energy is going towards trying to get Pat to express love and acceptance and tenderness. And that the great flow of Pat's energy is towards trying to maintain a feeling of control and safety and autonomy. These are first observations, obvious to some but not perhaps to Terry or Pat.

And, to continue, others can make the second observations that Terry is afraid of being deserted by Pat and that Pat is afraid of being overpowered or swallowed alive by Terry. And that these two fears provide the energy for how each is acting within the couple.

When the relationship is looked at from this perspective, we see Terry reacting to Pat's distancing maneuvers, in other words, to Pat's way of maintaining autonomy: Terry feels slightly rejected and so makes a stronger effort at gaining Pat's love and tenderness. And Pat, feeling more anxious and under pressure, tries harder to keep a neat, separate world where Terry cannot enter. This is a knot that tightens itself on being pulled.

As a tightened knot, the relation is structured to teach WHAT?

Each has a chance here, especially if we imagine the attraction and the energy involved here to be great, to see an important aspect of themselves and of one another. There is a golden opportunity for the two to learn about an important fear each has, and how it frustrates the desire of each for contact.

I take it that this is an extremely valuable lesson about themselves, and about one another, for the two to learn.

(This lesson will *not* be learned if the two feel that the only issue is, after all, simply whether to live together or not, and conclude, "No, it's better not to," and let the whole thing drop then and there!)

Terry may come to see in looking further, for example, what his acting on the fear of rejection brings about when the other person responds by becoming more distant or colder. And Pat may come to see what his trying to keep well separated from another brings about when the other person responds by driving for more closeness.

57

These are important *first* lessons. The two may well learn the ways in which they experience frustration arising out of their ways of reacting that are typical or "characteristic" or so-called "natural" (speaking here of a conditioned pattern: one's "second nature").

And if they (or we) continue to look to see what there is to learn from the relationship, each may come to learn about these fears that constrict and frustrate.

When these fears are stimulated or triggered off by something in the relationship, we (or they) are in a prime position to look into these fears. Often, however, the fear is so strong that we do not find the breathing space to look at it until later. Whenever we can see it is when we can look into what it is about.

FEELING FEAR: there is a movement away from, as an arrow flying into the distance. In going along with fear, we follow the fleeing arrow. If we notice this flight, we may criticize this with an "Oh! We shouldn't have fear!"

This is getting into moralizing. Now, psychologically on the other hand, this fear is a clear indication of something important to us. We can feel that there is something valuable that is being threatened. So what is important to us here? (Flying with the fear can make it more difficult for us to get in touch with what we feel is important here.)

Fear keeps us running. It can put us in a very tight and anxious state of being. When we give ourselves the time and enough room to breathe a little, we can come to know this fear and the related important concern this fear is threatening.

So we can come to see that this fear is based on some strong desire or preference of ours. Terry's fear of being rejected, for example, depends on the desire not to be alone. And Pat's fear of being swallowed depends on the desire to make still and constant what actually feels very shaky, wobbly, insecure. Now this looking at *the root desires that underlie fear* leads to appreciating our own life *experiences* that have deeply marked us, which can lead to compassion for and understanding of ourselves.

And this can give the confidence to look further. (Without confidence, fear is hard to transcend. Hard, not impossible.) Looking further, we come to see what the fear's root, this strong desire, is *itself* resting on. The desire not to be alone, for example, rests on Terry's discomfort at being alone. (This relates, in our example, to powerful experiences in Terry's *past* of anxious and painful aloneness, which condition and perpetuate this *present* fear.) This sense of discomfort may be gone into and through and beyond in pure contemplation, but *it may take the lived reality* of being alone *for Terry to come face to face with what is uncomfortable* about that for him. (There is also an EERIE attraction to what we fear because we all know just this painful truth!)

One way or another, fear can be seen through. We can see, with investigation or consideration, its intimate relation to our desires and to our wanting to protect ourselves! Imagine learning what self-image is driving us and keeping us the slave of this fear! The key here is an open curiosity about what this self-image really involves us in: how in our *experience* it structures what we will do or think, and what we will not do or think, how we will feel and not feel, when we will be at ease and when anxious. We can experience how this self-image, a little mental creation we recall from time to time, gives us work and worries, in exchange for a cramped island of apparent safety. (We may feel a need to watch out that it doesn't sink, or get invaded, or even lost.) Then we are seeing in reality how we truly feel when deeply identifying with or clinging to or being saddled with a given fear-generating self-image. When we do *that* enough, it will be time to just let it all drop! ! !

Until we get to these roots of the fear in our desires and self-concerns and images, we do not fully see or experience or understand this fear. When we *do* see these roots and work through what they do for us, when we are no longer boxed in by what they "help" us avoid, then we *have* been thorough in our uprooting, and *have* worked through what they are about, they are finished for us, through, and we, being thorough, are thoroughly through: a Sanskrit chant celebrated this process beginning with the term gate, *pronounced not like the English monosyllabic word of this spelling, but in two syllables (as* ga-te*);* in full the chant is: gate (going), gate (going), pāragate (going through, past, and beyond), pārasamgate (going completely beyond).

When we are through in this way, this fear is no longer able to take root in us, or, we can recognize it quickly if it does. Then the fear cannot drive us blindly along as it had been doing up until then. At this stage in our learning about and "working through" our conditioning (our "second nature") — and thus coming to our "third nature"* — we can see the fear arise, see what triggers it off, and simply let it be, not having it lead us even one little bit, totally inconsequential, neither binding nor frustrating.

This is freedom from specific fears through working through their roots in our self-imposed strictures created by our karma, our past actions and reactions to life's situations. When these strictures/structures are seen and let be to burn out ("burning karma": karma which is burning out), we have seen ourselves and our fears and their end. And it is each specific relationship that can show us ourselves and our fears. (And can show us all the rest, too, of course.)

We can say here that each such relationship then gives us the key to freeing ourselves a little. This is when relationship frees us from our self-defeating patterns: because of this specific feature these are spoken of in some traditions as liberating relationships.

The self-discovery that underlies this becoming free is most powerful when there is a strong and undeniable attraction between the two in spite of these self-defeating, or rather, frustrating, patterns. This strong attraction — different from romantic love (with its saccharine sweet, always harmonious, free of tensions or frustrations, somewhat bland, rather predictable, stereotypically "happily ever after" nature) — becomes a spotlight that makes it possible to see the frustrating patterns in greater highlight than usual. It may be used in order to see these patterns more deeply, and to go more fundamentally beyond them.

This attraction is in this way spiritual, liberating. Do you remember when we were troubadours, and would pass the word about this liberating force by singing of Spiritual Love?

---

* For a discussion of our third nature, see Chapter 13 ("The Second Transformation: Our Third Nature & Recalibration") in M. Ginsberg, *Calm, Clear, and Loving: Soothing the Distressed Mind, Healing the Wounded Heart* (Second edition, 2012), pp. 211-214.

I LOVE YOU

I love you where there is no language: in the silence where we two see all realities in their flow. We look together and see what is going by and accept all there is to accept, which is, all there is, all. If we touch by means of the body-sense, it is not *in order to* BECOME close: we are already as one: we have already been through some of the same spaces of consciousness. We have looked at each other, and seen — beyond all manifestation, beyond each moment of consciousness — the other, resting open and loving, fully accepting, fully understanding, fully feeling, sensing, and thinking. We look at each reality as it is, not belonging to anyone — even thoughts of "This is mine." You bring to me, for me to see, a light of life, and there is joy in the seeing of this visible energy. The light is ownerless. It goes through "our" awareness: you are illuminating, my shining being, my deva, and you are neither within nor without. In joy and love I lower my head towards you, and I say, "Namas te."

Nāga-Buddha-rūpa
XI-XIVth Century
Lopburi Style
Thailand

TO THE BELOVÈD

To The Belovèd, Ishq'allah, Krishna, Holy YOU
I live in YOU breathe me

       in
       and out
       and in I live through YOU nourish me
              YOUR energy

gives me life I grow in joy
       feeling YOU in me, YOU
          before me, YOU
          around me, YOU

YOU

    are limitless
      energy itself
      life in form
        in flow
           changing
           growing
           evolving
              the beauty of life.

THIS totality-in-movement
    full
        answering all demands effortlessly
           with what already manifests
              YOU.

HEART-FELT THINKING

Breathing is on-going: at times it is shallow, at times deep; at times brief, at times long; sometimes silent, and other times audible. Watching these changes, we are continually aware of our body. If we keep feeling the expansion and contraction in our chest area, where the lungs are filling and emptying, we are more in touch with our body's relation to what is happening at each moment.

It's all in the breathing. Being grounded in movement, non-statically, comes with experiencing the present reality through our bodies. An aspect of this is being in constant touch with how our bodies are. When there is a tightness in the heart area, constricting breathing, for example, something is tension-producing in the moment. We can experience such a tension without rejecting our experience, without trying to make our bodies relax, when we simply notice the tension, accepting it fully, welcoming it as highlighting for us some dissatisfaction.

Or perhaps the breathing is slow and deep. Do we see the ease in the moment? Then we can be fully alive to the harmonious situation.

At times we are experiencing life from within our heart area. At other times, we are trying to figure out what is happening. The latter gives us headaches, especially above or in the eyes, while the former centers us with heart-felt awareness. So, staying with our heart area, we are not channeling our life's energies here into cerebral processes; we are simply feeling with our full being what is happening. This is not constricting the depths of our "being in touch with reality" to what we can comprehend, can understand, but giving full reign to all of our prowess as sentient beings.

Then there is a clearly experienced harmony between our thinking and our full feeling. We can call this thinking with the heart, heart-felt thinking.

As you breathe in
    as you breathe out
        when there is no breathing —
    what's happening in your heart?

64

ANGER AND ILL WILL

Sometimes we would rather believe anything than acknowledge certain realities or experience certain emotions. We want life to be pleasant. We retract from tensions and from what we fear will be painful. We complicate our lives at times in this attempt at peacefulness.

We want not to be upset. We want things not to bother us. We want not to get riled up. This leads to a frustration when we start to become upset, when things do begin to bother us.

We don't want to cause waves. We don't want to confront others. We'd like to be a nice chap or a nice lady. We swallow our irritation, our annoyance, our resentment. We try to feel pure and above anger. Afraid to face our emotions, afraid to express our displeasures, afraid to stand up for ourselves, we hide behind the distorting self-image of an evolved or spiritual or holy being. We talk of the sin or of the "unskillful" nature of ill will, of anger. Inside we seethe with rage, or stew in irritation. Outside we are very pleasant, indeed. This is not evolved or spiritual or holy. It is simply putting on a façade that makes it more devious for us to come to see ourselves as we truly are.

We might feel that anger is agitating and unpleasant, and believe that it ought to be suppressed, or that we should be above it. Or we might feel that anger is healthy, and believe that it ought to be expressed, or that we should get into our anger and encourage it along.

What I have noticed is that on some occasions anger is expressed, even explosively, and that nonetheless it is not cleaned out by this process. And on other occasions, anger is not expressed but dealt with in a complete way even so. I feel that the essential issue is not whether we get into being demonstrative in our anger or not, but whether we recognize the anger, acknowledge it readily, and experience it, its roots, its manifestations, all fully and consciously, or not.

In anger we can experience a visceral and emotional response to something that infringes on our freedom of action or on our sense of well being. Anger itself, we can see, is the manifestation of a stand in the world. This may be lauded or criticized or may simply be seen for what it actually is.

In ill will we can experience a mental attitude. Perhaps we can see the frustration or sadness underlying this critical mentality, which may itself be focused or may be diffusely applied against whatever comes to our attention. It frequently feels rancorous or festering within us. We may come to appreciate that not acknowledging and consciously experiencing anger may result in a build-up of ill will and resentment. In Pāli, this state is described by the word paṭigha (Sanskrit, pratigha), who literal meaning is striking (-gha) back against (paṭi-, prati-). Some of you may perhaps be reminded here of Nietzsche's incisive words on *ressentiment*, this all-too-common phenomenon of impotent rage (as in *Genealogy of Morals*, Part I).

If there is anger, we have the possibility of feeling the energy of this state, the feeling that accompanies it of groundedness or agitation, of confidence or cowardice.

If there is ill will, we can see what it is which we find unacceptable, what we want to be different, what we resent. Here we have the opportunity to see how ill will arises, how it affects our thoughts, our responses to others, our bodies. We can see the critical orientation it gives to our perception, and the bitter flavor it gives to our experience.

When we get inside anger, or inside ill will, not to identify with them: "Oh, that's what I'm like," but simply to experience the phenomena occurring to us, we can learn more about ourselves, about our desires and their frustrations, and about how we deal with those unhappy realities. And we can see when they go, how they go, whether we chase them away, suppress them, or whether we allow them to show themselves fully to us, be heard, and leave of their own accord when finished.

LIVING THROUGH FEAR

It's all changing. That's nothing new. But even how it's all changing feels different — the magnitude of changes is increasing, isn't it, all over the world. Impermanence, or anicca, even in anicca. Now we can experience not only velocity, change through time, but also acceleration, changes in change through time! And where is it all going?

Things seem to many to be beyond control, to be heading rapidly in a disastrous direction. Species seem to be dying off almost daily. Anyone who reads a newspaper or tunes in to a news program even occasionally is almost painfully aware of such trends. We may even have the impression that all of this is ever more the case as we consider these past several decades that have recently come and gone.

In times like this, there will be much fear to experience. Fear leads to freezing up, to searching for safety, to fantasies of better days gone by: nostalgia, perhaps to high circus by way of manicked avoidance of the "heavies" of the great pain all around, lurking almost everywhere. There is much more to fear than fear itself, as any sampling of people in fear will show.

Fear rests on confusion, and on ego concerns. Its drive is towards unseeing action, wherever that might lead from the particular situation in which it arises. Its overcoming is through patience: the patience to remain where the fear is, to accept the confusion, the unseeing, and to keep on the path, to keep on watching at every moment to see better into this not-yet-clear, problem-filled reality.

This isn't a nice matter of the "perfecting of one's pāramīs or one's pāramitās" as part of any idealized diversion, but of coming full-face to grips with what we wish were different.

We can see into fear by looking at what is easy to observe — perhaps this is day-dreaming's wishes and imaginings. Through these we can experience how we conceive or imagine a "better" reality to be. If we allow the imagination full reign, and look into what most appeals to us, we can continue to see, through this extreme, what least appeals to us in this present situation, experienced as itself horrible or as implying some horrible future.

In any case, there is no choice here. The present is what it is. Greatly difficult times are times of great opportunity for gaining in understanding, in patience, in love, in magnanimity. In Buddhist terms, it is through suffering through all of Mankind's woes that the way out of each and every one of them is seen, and thereby can a bodhisattva be of deepest aid to all other sufferers. The bodhisattva vow to save an infinite number of beings from suffering is a wonderful but so deep, so immense a commitment when what it truly involves is appreciated. Homage to all Buddhas, to all Arahats, homage to all Bodhisattvas, and homage to all of us.

FROM FEAR TO OPEN FRIENDSHIP

We all want love and the good companionship of others, at least occasionally. Or, at least many people will readily admit to such desires.

Is there anyone who would not like warm, loving feelings, caring about one another, being alive to the joys and sorrows of friends, being filled with love, admiration, concern, good-will?

Yet, even so, this isn't the way it always turns out. In spite of our desires.

Why is this so? We may have the good fortune to be able to share the open company of others. Can we look, though, when it happens, to see what gets in the way of this easy sharing?

Are we alert enough to hear what the other is saying, not so much in the words, but deep down? Do we realize how the other is feeling, what frame of mind he or she has at the moment?

Perhaps we do. Yet we still might find, much to our dismay or at least to our surprise, that we seem to turn quickly away from this appreciation of the other to a less intimate, less in-touch awareness, and so, to a less intimate, less in-touch communication.

We may begin debating with what was said. Or we may simply express our understanding or appreciation of what is being talked about.

Or we may go from that appreciation to some old situation that the present reality brings to mind.

Are we aware that our body has pulled back from our companion? That it is getting more tensed?

Have we returned to our own reality? Was this simply keeping centered, or non-distracted? Or perhaps we notice an element of distance from the other person, of wanting to make sure that it's clear to everyone, especially to ourselves, how we think, how we feel — in short, who we are.

So this concern to stay in touch with ourselves may limit our openness to others.

The way out of this is not through developing self-hatred because we are closed off to others.

What there is to see is this: a feeling of insecurity, of being unsure of ourselves, of wanting to be assured of who we are. Do we look below these uneasy feelings, to see what they rest on?

Can we see fear at all? Fear about who we are? (There can be such fear even if there is no "me," no "you.") We may experience this as a fear, worry, minor concern, occasional issue, that others won't like us, won't like who we are, won't like what they "know" of us, won't like what they see of us.

This can show itself at other times when we notice ourselves worrying about what to wear, or how we look ("Do I look O.K., honey?"), or in other ways.

We can look into this type of fear and so meet up with our ideas about what we should be like, and trembling nervously behind this, our ignorance or false "knowledge" about who we are. Once we can see the self-image that we are taking to be a worrisome and unacceptable reality, once we can see who it is we fear we really are, we can begin looking through this image — first, to see how it is influencing, perhaps even controlling, our thoughts, our actions, much of our life's energies; and then, to see its roots.

Uprooting cannot occur unless force is applied at the base of the tree. And so, this crippling pattern cannot be uprooted unless we are at its base. But as it does get uprooted, we go naturally from fear to open friendship.

Can you taste the sweet fruits of this investigation? Can you feel, right now at this moment, the worth of this digging? Acknowledging this feeling deeply will give energy to the investigation; the only tool required is timely attentiveness to ourselves in each of the situations life provides for us.

THE PEACEMAKERS

It is said in the Sermon on the Mount (Matthew 5), blessèd are the peacemakers. The passage continues, for they will be called the children of God (at Matthew 5:9). Why is this?

We have all had the occasion to experience people who want to fight, to argue, to insult, even to slander or to harm others physically.

That may be exciting, of course, whether pleasant or unpleasant; it may be invigorating, having us feeling the adrenalin coursing through our bodies. But we also almost surely are aware of the intended hurtfulness and the actual hurt that are present in those contexts.

When will we have enough of initiating this sort of interaction, when we will have enough of entering into it in response to some affront or attack, real or simply sensed, felt, or imagined? When will we have enough of such turbulent, ill-willed ways of interacting with other?

When will allow the development and full fruition of our natural inclinations to live in harmonious good will with one another?

DIGGING, DISCOVERING

A favorite sutta (discourse of the Buddha) of my teacher, Dhiravamsa, has been the Ant-hill Sutta. In this discourse, the young man described there, representing a meditator, keeps digging, day and night, as a metaphor for an ongoing, thorough investigating of consciousness. In this activity, he encounters a number of objects, each of which represents one feature of another of conscious process, in the aim of discovering or coming to, developing, wisdom.

This investigation into our own consciousness is more than a matter of noticing each moment one after the other.

As a first intensification or expansion of our consciousness beyond simply being "in the present," noticing what is present in awareness now, and now, and now, one moment after the next, in what can be a very lucid, clear, inspiring, and powerful way (in what has been recently called the power of now), we begin to see the inter-connectedness of various moments or features of our consciousness: the co-arising, for example, of an unpleasant experience with a mind that is criticizing or finding fault, or with a tension or aching in some part of our body; or the co-arising of awareness of a groaning sound in someone nearby and our sadness at that (perhaps minor) torment, perhaps with a wish for that suffering to end, in other words, for that person to be free of discomfort, pain, or anguish.

This already has us notice and appreciate the inter-connected web of our consciousness, as it presents itself to our attentive mind (to our awareness).

In a further dimension of this ongoing, evolving enhancement of our understanding of nāma-rūpa, that is, of the mind-body complex as an integrating system in process, we may begin to sense, perhaps to intuit, to appreciate, to perceive, and, at times, to understand clearly, calmly, and with gentle compassionate good will (loving) what has us think and speak and act as we do.

This may involve years of meditation before it happens, or with a background of no formal meditation at all, but when it does happen, it can come into clarity in a very short time, in seconds or minutes. To ground any such particular seeing-into-process, it will often help to stay with it, to savor the particular interconnected parts, and in this, we may come to sense or to recognize what is the underlying driving motivation in our thought, speech, and actions.

We may perhaps see that we are kind and helpful in part, at least, because of a desire to be appreciated and treated gently, in turn.

We may see that we are sharply, subtly, and intelligently critical and attacking because of an anger at some kind of behavior we are now criticizing, and recognize the link between this and our having been mistreated by someone earlier in our lives in this same way.

Whatever the particulars, having seen these apparent underlying (and often non-acknowledged) mind-sets guiding or directing our way of being in the world, we can next see how we respond to these mind-sets.

We may feel embarrassed, or ashamed, about them. We may then see a justifying mind come to the diversionary defense of this shame or embarrassment. We may become angry at ourselves to see the uncomfortable power of the given mind-set that we are now recognizing.

Of course anger at ourselves is one way our urge to be different can manifest itself. If we see the underlying ideal we are yearning for, wishing to be more that way, that energy can be used to fuel just such an invitation to ourselves to continue in the envisioned way, more skillful, less noxious or pain-creating.

It is a gradual lifetime path.

WE'RE ANGRY

We're angry
at others now for
how we fear we might become,
or sense vaguely, or clearly,
that we once were.

We see all of the torment, the dukkha,
our worries about who we really are lead to.
Attempts at self-definition too are
passing mental processes,
arising out of specific particulars, this or that.
No reason to clutch on to these attempts,
these patterns.
We let go; we let them go by.
No self; no worry about self-image.

Self-image: mirage of a delusion.

No self-image;
no fears, worries, anxieties about who we are.

Time to end self-doubt is
when the issue of self and self-definition
or essential nature arises,
whenever it arises,
then and there.

WE CAN BE FEELING

We can be feeling how people are rather than merely understanding
what they (their words) are saying.
The mind's limit is the imagination; the heart's, fear.
If I misunderstand you, I end up confusing myself.
The mind's knowing is knowledge; the heart's, understanding.
In deep relationship comes fullness of heart not fullness of self.

THE PASSIONATE BUDDHIST
(BEYOND BOREDOM)

There are *levels* of "open mindfulness": Have we allowed ourselves to feel our own depths, the degree to which we are capable of resonating in harmony with our environment? Do we appreciate our own richness?

When we let go of our controlling, and let our situation, and ourselves in that situation, become fully intermeshed, we are in for the experiences of our lives! All of this is extremely powerful: to be completely alive is the farthest thing from boredom there is.

As we let go, either bit by bit, aspect by aspect, level by level, or radically, all at once — watch what happens.

We stop demanding to know everything in advance. We are no longer sure of where things will go before they go there. We have no solid footing.

But we still have awareness of where things are when they are there (here). We can see our own reactions to our not feeling in control. We know in our heart and in our gut how we feel at the moment.

Here we just appreciate how our changing situation is making us feel, and what we do here in dance, in interaction, with our situation.

We see into our moods. Once controlled and moderated, they may well look like ocean swells where once there were only creek ripples. It's all full of vitality. We do not have to adjust this, to get back to a "middle path."

Our fully experiencing each swell ends at the leveling out and ending of each swell. Or did we take on the idea that unless we ended a feeling it would just go on forever? Then we will be surprised by its ending on its own.

In this continual alertness and full allowing acceptance of our being and reacting, whatever they are like, there is a great stability. This is not the stability of a tin man at attention, but of a ripe, mature, flexible human who can feel (*ein echter Mensch*: a *real* human).

Once we know what it is to be fully alive, the model of an individual who takes care never to do anything ("Watch out that you don't create any more karma") and who is neutral to everything that happens ("Be without desire") has little appeal. Why choose a puddle-life when life's energies are oceanic?

What a joy to be alive. What wonders are life itself, consciousness and awareness, contact between living beings! How magnificent when we dare to live fully, to be open to all of reality (not merely to what fits our model of some "correct" or even "enlightened" life).

Here we feel creative, light, flexible, alert, energized, clear, open to life's possibilities. We are no longer fasters at the feast.

We thrive on the changes we experience. We see how reality moves on, coming to fruition effortlessly when we do not try to hold it back. Each stage goes deeply through us. We *live* through each, fully, deeply.

Full living is not for the weak-hearted!

DIGGING AND DIGGING

Here we return to a discourse, sometimes called the sutta on the ant-hill (discussed above at pages 72-73, in the chapter "Digging, discovering"), in which the advice is repeatedly given to keep on digging; literally, digging into the ant-hill; metaphorically, some other sort of digging, of course.

What is the digging that we are be involved in here, and for how long are we to go on digging?

The digging is our investigation into consciousness. In this process, we keep noticing one thing after another.

Leaving behind the discourse (sutta) in question here, we can perhaps recognize the value of continuing our investigation of what arises in our minds, not stopping or delaying at any particular moment of consciousness, but not skipping over and disregarding what is presenting itself to our awareness, moment after moment.

When we notice the particulars of our thinking, judging, feeling of a pleasant, or of an unpleasant, moment, our memories, associations, fears, frustrations, irritations, angers, and on and on, we may begin to notice some patterns. And we may begin to notice what is in some obvious way the basic state of mind that is the foundations of these patterns of thinking and feeling and such.

If we stay attentive to these experienced particulars, we may come to great insights into their inter-connected, complex nature, or at least into some of their prominent features, as we are impressed by them in our practice of being ongoingly mindful.

If we keep on digging at such times, beginning to see the same particulars or the same patterns repeating, perhaps over and over again, and look to see what all of this turbulence in consciousness is reflecting, which state of mind is underlying, is in the background of it all, we may come to some great realizations.

As an example, we may think of some interaction that is bothering us a great deal, one that will not feel settled and resolved, no matter how long and how detailed our search for insight and understanding.

Perhaps someone has done something we do not like. Or has not done something we would have liked, or expected, that person to do.

So we may think over the details of the interaction that led to what we thought was an agreement. And we may see where the other person either did not understand correctly (meaning: as we understood it all), or what that person did that went against what we were expecting or hoping for, or both. We can be focused on judging those actions or non-actions or on judging the person, on the basis of that interaction and the features we are focusing on.

We can consider what we might do to correct things, to bring things back into balance, to create justice or fairness, or in some other way come to some resolution that we find happy or pleasant.

If at such points we can look to see what is the issue for us underlying all of these considerations, we may come to a grander, more inclusive vision and appreciation not only of the situation but of what is actually important to us in the situation.

So, if instead of staying with thoughts and considerations that lead to the conclusion that the other person is mean, or insensitive, or a criminal, or untrustworthy, or ..., we may come to see that we are agitated and upset, in this imaginary example, by our sense of being betrayed.

If this is what we come to notice in a shift from the details of the story or situation, in our digging and digging, our continuing with our investigation of the particulars of this present experience, we may open up a gold mine, or perhaps a golden mountain, of understanding of what is important to us at this specific time in our lives.

If we continue on here so that we are now coming to see and have the opportunity of investigating what this sense of betrayal is like — to continue the example — we may come to appreciate what the agitation concerns that we are experiencing and that is driving our thinking, perhaps in this case, judgmental thinking. And in this, we can go from staying with thoughts of what the other person's faults or misdeeds and such are to encountering our own personal needs and concerns. Here, we would begin to glimpse the importance for us of the issue of a betrayal by another.

If we do this and now continue digging on even more, so that we can come to see the meaning in our life of betrayal, what it represents or reminds of us from our past, what its resonances are for us in our sense of who we are, or what our relationships are like, or

78

what we need and feeling that we will never receive, or whether there is reason or hope that we will ever have the kind of relationship we are missing at this time, with another person. So in this we can see the tendency of the mind to go from some particular situation to a sense that it will always, or will never, be a certain way. This can lead to a sense of hopelessness.

But it can also lead to a realization that there is something at this time that is very important for us, that we are giving a great deal of importance to the idea of some sort of relationship with others, or with some one special, specific other. In this case, we may notice the importance we give to a relationship with deep trust, one in which we sense that the other will treat us with respect, will give our interests value in thinking, considering, and acting, most importantly, where it may have an impact on us, our lives, our experience.

In general, it is through the carrying on digging, from each particular, appreciating it, understanding it, but continuing on to see what is still important to see but not yet seen, that we can dig to the very depths of our particular mind and its patterns.

All of this is leading, step by step, particular digging to particular digging, to a compassionate understanding, a compassionate insight, into ourselves.

THE HEART PULLS US ON

The heart pulls us on to live.
How can we refuse it?
By being heartless.

Half-hearted, I rest alone. It is only a transient stage.
My fulfillment lies in the summer of rebirth,
when I become you.
'Til then I am jealous most of all of you,
who are always close to you.

How does the heart open?

Sometimes it's so intense, with chest-shaking sobbing.
Breathless tightness and its explosive release.
A deep relaxing in the chest, through the body.
A glowing peace, a bathing in the heart's golden radiance.
All-open calm, the full body and mind
floating, buoyant in sweet ease.

Sometimes it is a very easy and non-strained
and gentle process:
like the melting of snow on a warm spring day.

The heart pulls us on to live.
How can we refuse it?
By being heartless.

THE STINGY HEART

The heart without a feeling of love, with no joy, is so sad. But, still, we can bear to look at it. Then we can see what it is to feel without love.

"Oh, I am so worthless. No one likes me. Or at least, no one with any reasonable values likes me." We can note that in this state of mind we feel unworthy, and we expect others to feel the same towards us. We look down, or away, unwilling to look at the hatred we think we would see if we looked. So our feeling of isolation increases by our taking this passing thought, feeling, this expectation, to be reality.

We can notice that we tighten the chest, or pull the head down and in to close the chest, or bring the shoulders forward, or cramp the belly space. All this makes us feel non-expansive, cramped, and uncomfortable on the physical level. And the feeling on the psychological or emotional level is no different, is it?

I want to hold on to the little love I feel. So we do just that. Stingy with love.

If we have little money and we hoard it, at least it won't diminish.

And if we do give it away, we *will* have less than the little we began with.

When we act this way with our feeling little love, we can see, we can experience, that love is very unlike money.

The more we close our love in, the less love we feel, the less love we *have*.

When *do* we feel love in our hearts? Is it when love is coming in to our empty heart? If we feel a lack of love in our hearts, love coming in to us may only make us feel worse, or, more numb. "Oh, *they* are so loving; I am so much colder than they are." That's thinking typical of such a frame of mind, isn't it?

Do we feel love in our hearts when we are possessive about love, when we grab and clutch at whatever love comes to us? When we want and feel a need for love, and love comes to us, is it *ever* enough? Do we feel that the *stinginess* of love is in the *other* person, the one being loving towards us?

This may lead us to *demand* love: to feel this desire and this need for more love, and to think that others, or certain particular others, *ought* to give it to us, or, at least to hope and to pray that these others *will* give us this love.

We want others to give us love; we want to hold on tight to the little love we feel; we think that this will bring us peace.

The stingy frame of heart with its demand for a favorable balance of trade in the love market will not reach peace.

So, again let us ask, when *have* we felt love in our hearts? We can look here into our own experiences. How have we felt towards others at such times? We can see that the more love we gave out towards others, the *larger* our own heart felt, the warmer.

Yet, following the mechanical rule or idea "Give love to others to feel love in your heart" is to give ourselves a task, an obligation. This may well lead to feelings of failure, resentment, anger, rancor, bitterness. *We can't mechanically give love.* If it flows forth, it flows forth. If it doesn't, we can see that it doesn't. And if it doesn't, then there's an obstacle to the flow here.

The place to look for greater love in our hearts isn't especially in how we are lovable, especially when we feel unlovable. At such times we can still look to see what touches our heart about those we have contact with.

This takes going beyond ourselves. When we feel so miserable, the tendency is often to shut off to everything outside ourselves. So we can gently lift our awareness, with good-willed energy, to the rest of reality at such times.

Here is a subtle but powerful practice for us.

What will we experience then? Sadness? Anger? Fear? Love? If we look, we will appreciate our relatedness to the rest of reality and how that relating is working, and how it is all resonating in our hearts.

This practice is a simple way to intensify our sense of connection, of caring, and of compassionate love, an antidote to the stingy heart.

THE BITTER HEART

The bitter heart, suffering in rancor, will not let things go, will not let go of rage, resentment, an urge to strike back at what it feels is causing its pain, or to relieve its anguish.

"Oh, they have wronged me!" "I do not deserve this!" "They will pay for this — for what they have put me through in their heartlessness!" "This will help make things even." And so forth.

The heart suffering in rancor senses a poison, a great lack of ease (or dis-ease, as some say), a malaise.

Misidentifying its source and its nature, misjudging it to be outside themselves, those with such rancor strike out in a wild, even vicious, attempt to destroy what they take to be the source of their troubles, their torment.

In this, what they are doing is creating more torment, without this going to the heart of the matter — to something that they are not digesting well in their lives, either in their present situation or in their own personal history and its share of dukkha.

Of course, we do not eliminate our own dukkha by being the source of anguish, annoyance, hurt, fear, and other responses that others may feel in response to these ways we might express our bitterness and our frustration, our rage and our resentfulness.

Once again, by facing what our own original hurts were, we can come to resolution about them. This is called the overcoming of conditioning and is a powerful process if we allow ourselves to enter into these murky, often filthy waters, to come to appreciate with compassion what has actually happened, refraining from distracting ourselves now with bitter rage at others that have little or nothing to do with the source of our torments.

THE ENVIOUS HEART

The envious heart, wishing it had what another has, will not be content with what is or with what it feels is possesses.

From a deep sense of not having what is wanted, or longed for, when this is seen elsewhere, we do not experience a vicarious joy for those involved, but, instead, feel a dissatisfied agitation for what we take this to mean about ourselves.

This often leads to a very critical mind, attempting to undermine the worthiness of those who are enjoying what is felt to be lacking but strongly yearned for by us.

We see someone who can accomplish some physical feat. We do not stay in appreciation of this accomplishment. We do not clearly acknowledge that we would like to be able to do that as well. We focus on how this person has some faults we can criticize, to belittle a person we might otherwise take as a model or inspiration for our own endeavors.

The same happens if we see someone enjoying some happiness we want ourselves, but are suffering from not having. Perhaps we see Jesse who we wish would want to be with us, who is instead spending time with Ell. We are envious of Ell who has the company of Jesse, for whom we long. We stay and intensify our sense of deprivation, critical in our nastiness, often doing so feeling justified and righteous in our perspective.

THE JEALOUS HEART

The jealous heart, suffering in a fear of loss, will not be content with what is.

Seeing here and there, perhaps everywhere, the possibility that we will lose what we have, we become guarded and angered when we sense something is threatening our possession.

We may see this when we are talking about relationships.

We are insecure in our connection with Kelly and sense, or fear with no particular grounds in the current situation, that we may lose that connection.

If we see Kelly speaking to or smiling at (or with) Morgan, we may sense our worry, imagining that Kelly will abandon us forever and want to be with Morgan instead. So we may demand that Kelly not speak to Morgan or even look at Morgan. And if Kelly does, we may feel angry and betrayed.

This fear of loss can be quite driven and tormenting, and lead to great frustration on everyone's part, especially, here, for us and for Kelly.

SOFT ARE YOUR WAYS

Soft are your ways
and loving.
Few are your words but full of truth,
spoken from the heart.
Gentle and shy
I feel you reach out,
gingerly,
with love.
You are precious to me
My friend.

PHYSICAL LOVE

Touching.
Holding.
Cuddling.
Breathing
as one.
Flowing motion;
full harmonies.
Bodies
in
music-less dance,
neither leading,
both alive with
movement.
Rhythms
of the
Universe.
Mystical
Union.

DEATH-CANAL LIFE-THROWS

Not enough air. Gasping. Still not enough. One of these exhalations will be followed by no inhalation! Sensation will go slowly, little by little, then blindness, numbness, deafness, death: Wait!!

So long as the task is to keep away the full face of death, when this body will cease inhalations, will take its last sigh, and respire no more — so long will this work have to fail, *some* day.

What is it to be about to die and say, "Wait!! I can't die yet!"? When the child is moving down between your legs and the muscles from the top of your head are flowing down in stepwise contractions toward your toes, what is it to try to stop that? And what, when your bowels want to empty themselves and in their contractions force whatever masses there are within them down toward and through their opening, what is it to try to stop that!

Childbirth and defecating could be lessons — the latter much more frequently available — on how to see that those processes which are occurring are simply occurring. Imagine facing death with that seeing!

As has been said by some, the important thing in life is to learn how to die. Now, since bravery is a bold front in face of something terrifying, this lesson is not: "Learn to die bravely"; but, rather: "Learn not to need to die bravely."

MEMORY IN THE PRESENT

Sometimes old memories are a gentle reminder, if we do not refuse them full entry into our consciousness, of some past still burning at our soul/psyche/mind/being. The advice to "Let go," to "Stay in the present," is well-intentioned as a balance against incessant obsessing. But this "Be here now!" advice can sway over gently, or not gently, into "Cut off thoughts of the past!" Then it has become still one more means of repression, of trying to censor certain awarenesses from our consciousness. If we can allow the past's reappearance in, when it shows up, we are not clinging to it, but we are also not expending energy in fighting to push the memory out of consciousness. Then we can see that this energy is otherwise usefully channeled into merely looking.

To let it be gone when it isn't there, but to learn as much as we can see when it does show up, feels like a gentle balance, don't you agree?

Some insistent memories are from times when it felt that things were happening too fast to take in, so that there were experience gaps. Recollection allows us to fill in these gaps so that they can truly be done with. In this process we notice an experiencing now of what earlier was too intense or too painful to live fully at the time. So we let ourselves move onwards at the rate we best operate at. There's no inner battle that has to be set up by turning this matter of moving onwards into an ideal about how to change. To accept our own rhythms, to appreciate them, is to see their divine beauty.

Do we fight memory ideas, or future-imagining ideas? I am reminded of some words from ages ago:

> If you wish to move in the One Way
>   do not dislike even the world of senses and ideas.
> Indeed, to accept them fully
>   is identical with true Enlightenment.

This rendering is based on the translation of Richard Clarke of a little talk called *Verses on the Faith Mind* (*Xìnxīnmíng* or *Hsin Hsin Ming*), by the third Zen Patriarch, Sēngcàn or Seng-ts'an (text title and author given in Pinyin and then in Wade-Giles transliteration).

THE PAST

What is the past? Perhaps it is all that has come and gone. All that has been and is now done with. Or that which lingers on, haunting us. Or that which keeps us from being newly alive at each moment.

We may feel that certain incidents in our lives will stay with us no matter how old we become. Or that certain patterns of acting are engrained in us until death. That we are nothing but the product of our past, perhaps of only our first few years.

Is the past what we are trapped in? Or perhaps the past is an old friend we return to for comfort and calm companionship — an alternative to the unfamiliar, the strange.

We all know remembering, the recalling of some event from the past. And then, an instant or an hour later, the jolting experience of snapping abruptly out of that memory.

So something is alive from the past, perhaps unsettled.

How do we treat this remembering when it occurs? We may just let it arise and come into awareness. Then it is merely noticed. When there is a memory-thought, there is just thinking. Or there may be a feeling of dissatisfaction that arises then, the feeling of having done something wrong. "Oh, I've lost it again! I think too much!" When we look back at what has been happening and respond this way, we are self-evaluating and criticizing ourselves.

If we can notice that there is some resistance to the natural, spontaneous process of having a memory arise, we can more clearly see what the memory is and what the resistance is. Is there just recollecting? Or does the command come to you, "Hey you! Be here now!" Have you taken on the rule not to remember anything? Then surely you will break your rule. A wise general never gives a command to the troops that they cannot carry out.

But perhaps we do want not to have any memories arise. And here, most definitely, a specific memory is coming up, anyway. So, once there was an experience and this is resulting now in something coming up in consciousness. We can look at this recollection with our present attentiveness, can see how it now affects us, how we have changed since that experience actually occurred. These recollections will give us material we can clear up from time to time.

When we see a memory arise, can we see it for what it is? We can acknowledge it to be a recollection while knowing the reality that it conjures up is no more. If we look carefully when a memory arises, we can see some feeling accompanying that memory: having the memory arise may be pleasant, or uncomfortable for us, or neutral. This feeling, whatever it is, is the key to the *present* status of the memory. So we must be quite attentive to noticing its flavor and texture. We can greatly increase our understanding if we stay with this accompanying feeling. It is stuffed with information for us about the present: it may be the recollection of some PAST event but it is a PRESENT recollection.

When we stay with this accompanying feeling, we appreciate its intensity. Perhaps it begins as a very weak feeling. Perhaps it has an even surface but develops strong undercurrents, say, of joy. Perhaps we see an inner satisfaction arise about what we have done. Can we accept this joy, this satisfaction? We can notice here the basis of this joy or satisfaction. Do we see what we are joyous or satisfied about, what about ourselves is pleasing or satisfying to us?

Or, as the memory ends, there may arise, for example, a bitter aftertaste. Is it clear then what is disagreeable to us? We can focus in here on what about the memory is unpleasant. We can see what sort of self we now reluctantly experience ourselves as. This memory is a remnant from a now-gone past. It may sit heavily on our shoulders and back. Perhaps returning to, being pained by this no-longer-existent "me" is like a habit we can't kick. Are we hooked on a nothing-but-remembered "me"?

Or perhaps we are free of this nothing-but-remembered "me." We are free not in the sense of denying that we did what we did, or that we felt what we felt. But at the same time we can appreciate that our PRESENT experience is not defined by the past.

So when a recollection arises, we do not have the attitude, "Yes! That's me!" — There is here neither attraction to the recollection nor aversion to it. We see it arise. We understand its basis, its roots. We know this to be the operation of memory. We know that this recollection can just go by. It is for us a bandwagon we feel no urge to jump onto. It does not make us feel superior to other people because we don't see ourselves in it. It is a ghost town with no one at home. Nor does it make us anxious or at all embarrassed. Why anxiety over some passing thought?

We do not delude ourselves into believing there is something to defend or praise about anyone in this process. It is simply a mental process, seen and understood for what it is in its bare nature.

Do you ever have this experience? Can you look for it now with mindful attentiveness? When we see things clearly this way, the world feels different. The ongoing flow is unobstructed and easy. There is a lack of heaviness. All of this is very agreeable.

That might be your experience of the past we call "ours." But we do not expect all others who have known us, or known of us, to have the same experience. Perhaps in one situation you find yourself free from the past, but the person you are with is talking to you as if you were defined by those earlier experiences and actions.

We can see in such a situation whether we are truly free from "our" past. That is, by meeting up with someone who is responding to our past, we can look to our own experience just now to check our own relation to that past. Do we feel annoyance? Perhaps we feel unappreciated in our present form, criticizing the other for not noticing us NOW. Are we free from the past in a way that makes us stuck in the present? We may feel an urge to bring the other up to date about us. This may simply be easy, open communication. Or it may be defensiveness, some form of lack of acceptance. If so, we can look into what about the situation we do not accept; what about the other's stale idea of us we find disagreeable.

People who are feeling that they already know us have a precon-ceived idea of how we act, what we will say, what we will feel. And this idea is at best an accurate overview of our past. Ideas from the past such as these roll onwards with a powerful momentum: this can control present experience if we are not quite attentive here. But we can use these ideas and their momentum to learn from. When we are approached by someone who has an idea of us from the past, we can have a liberating meditation. We recall the past they present us with. This does not require us to return to the past patterns at all; nor is letting the past come to us through others a matter of fatalism. We do not have the doctrine: it's my "karma" to live out this scene begun back then. We do not "live it out," for here this living it out would be no different from staying stuck in how we once might have been, or from being pulled back into that given pattern. We simply use the other's outdated ideas to help us see more clearly how much we have changed. *Mindfulness at such times is essential because of that tendency to return to these earlier painful patterns we call habits (our second nature) or our being in a rut.* Perhaps at such times this momentum of theirs will drag us back into what we were, *leading us into the temptation of acting habitually and blindly.*

This outcome, though, is not necessary. If we are mindful, we will first perhaps notice a difference between how we now feel about things and how the other takes us to be. This should be clearly noted with — and this is crucial — sufficient time spent in this difference to feel its full impact on us. The clearly and fully noting of this is quite powerful. *It can stop the shifting back into the old identity of ours that we are being presented with.*

Do we just let the disparity be between how we now feel and how we are seen? Or do we resist it? In order to stay out of a rut, we do not have to do anything, resist anything. All that is needed is *specific* refraining: *not taking* the next step in the old rut-sequence.

So we note the disparity. How long do we stay with this? When the situation arises, and you find yourself asking this question, then stay with this disparity a bit longer: see the full reality. And what is that reality? We feel that they have not noticed something, that they are not seeing us but just their own earlier-formed image of us. This means we feel there is not full true communication going on at this very moment, and that their ideas are obstructing their perception of the present reality. If so, can we let them have their slowness of perception? Can we let them use their past conceptions in the present? We feel the urge to help them to see with fresh vision.

But we don't have to keep the world up-to-date about the flow we experience. We can notice, however, whether this idea of bringing the other up-to-date about us has appeal to us. Do we see its roots? *Perhaps we feel that if we do not convince the other of how we are different, we will stop being convinced of the change ourselves.* Yes, this happens. We may well be afraid of slipping back into an old pain-producing style of ours. We feel that we have recently progressed, but we are shaky and unsure about this progress. This worry or doubt can be looked at. We know now that the way is simply to go on with mindful attentiveness to what is happening. So we can notice, as it begins, this fear of slipping back.

Now we meet up with someone who remembers an old us, and begins relating to us as that old us. We recognize the script. We have gone through this one before, we recall. Do we have stage-fright? Do we feel resistance to going through this again, a fear that we will get stuck in this role being re-assigned to us? Do we want to cut this off? to begin a new play? Perhaps we see a problem to tackle here: to define new conditions for our relating with this person from our past. Do we have an urge to sit down and set up a whole new contract before we go on to anything else? Are we becoming that worried about our slipping back? Let us see clearly. If we are tackling this problem, we are making things quite complicated for ourselves. It's not so hard for us, really: all we need is to stay with the ongoing reality. So we recognize this old script. And we see their interest in starting, anyway, on that familiar turf. We can accept this interest because we see freshly, in the moment, that it exists. We can unreservedly respond to that interest, with our full, fully-alive awareness. We will be allowing the old script but LIVING FULLY IN ATTENTIVENESS to the full *current* inter-action occurring between us and the other. For us it will be going into this realm for the first time. As we follow our ever-new awareness, the script subtly changes. We stay on this level. And if the other remains unaware of these subtle changes, our own contact with them is too clear to be blurred for us. This requires no fights, no arguments, no debate, no convincing. Surely with mindfulness and patience through time on our parts, the others will ultimately come along on their own, through their own observations.

In this way, the realization by others of how we are now differ-ent will come about simply through our own ongoing awareness of whatever is occurring between us and them. Mindfulness in us is noticeable by others as it flows along its own special way. Then they will experience the new us. This is triumph not through domineering, we are not conquerors; but triumph through ability to endure, through patience and non-belligerency. We let reality teach at its own rhythms.

THE DROSS OF SAD PASTS NOT YET GONE

Mourning grief remorse guilt nostalgia
all see the past with sad significance
inviting seeking, investigation
into our values, our heart.

The alchemy of using the dross
to derive the blessings,
appreciating and refining our life.

Perhaps ultimately seeing
            its perfect perfection
        (its Apollonian-beautiful stable perfection) *and*
            its perfect imperfection pushing us challenging us,
and through that further alchemy, ultimately embracing
            its reassuring wholeness *and*
            its question-raising cracks
        (its Wabisabi-beautiful limping living imperfection).

TURNING POISON INTO NECTAR

Here we return to the Buddhist concept of the peacock (presented above at pages 9-11, in the chapter "The Buddhist Peacock"), with a slightly different focus.

As in the earlier chapter, the peacock is taken as a metaphor for a wise person who is capable of going through what is harmful or poisonous to others, but to find value, to be able to integrate (swallow and digest) it, to be able to find nourishment (energy, inspiration, and so forth) in it.

How is this done? Here we will raise some specifics that are a complement to what was said above, with some examples to illustrate various approaches to specific mind-state situations.

One teaching invites the meditator *not* to react, that is, not to respond in a knee-jerk fashion in sensing that there is a poison, by the natural inclination to withdraw, to hide, to counter-attack, to become judgmental, to confront.

The alternative proposed is to recognize what this poison, this poisonous experience, leads to (for us), and to acknowledge what our resultant states of mind are. Are we hurt? angry? afraid?

We may find ourselves in some state of agitated mind, agitated by hurt, or fear, or anger, or perhaps a mixture of these and even other ingredients composing our experienced consciousness.

Keeping to the metaphor, we may realize that how to deal with a given poison depends on what the poison is.

Not all poisons call for the same antidotes.

So how we deal with a feeling of not being respected, or of being insulted, mocked, ignored, or attacked physically, and so on: each of these may call for a different response on our part.

In terms of finding nourishment in this process, a first step is to open up our natural curiosity, our natural desire to understand and to appreciate what is going on that is disturbing us.

If we sit on a something prickly (perhaps a burr), we naturally look to see what it is. Or if we sit on something soft that makes a sound of distress (perhaps a kitten), we at least look about. So, if we do not block our natural curiosity here, we look to investigate, even if only very briefly, to see what is going on. That is perhaps the most general first step that we may talk of here.

Here, with some poison that we sense is disturbing us, there is appreciating what our new agitation is based on.

Depending on what we realize here, our next steps may vary widely. We may walk away from the poisonous situation. Or we may stay and look inwards.

If the poison is in the form of something incidental or accidental, as when something bad happens to us, we might feed that incident by declaring that we always have bad luck. If the poison is in the form of words (criticism, blame), then we might judge ourselves to be even worse that what we are accused of! Or want to defend ourselves from some perceived injustice.

We have a chance here to look into our own sense of who we are. This is not only to see the simple self-image that is resonating and being activated for us, but also to see how it itself becomes a poison for all of our thinking at the time — and perhaps for days or longer, afterwards.

If we can free ourselves from this self-imposed prison, and in this open to the larger life context in which this particular poison has been injected, the many dimensions of this fuller reality of ours that we can become aware of, will put this moment of our lives into a much greater context, having us no longer disoriented from the flow of our life. This is allowing us to transform the initial poison into rich nourishment.*

* See also the discussions in "The Buddhist peacock" (pp. 9-11) and "Forgiving and recognizing new horizons" (p. 49). A number of these particular states of mind are investigated and presented for careful consideration in M. Ginsberg, *Peace and War and Peace: The Heart in Transformation Heart* (Second edition, 2015).

POWER OF THE NOW, PRISON OF THE NOW

The power of the now imprisons in the now,
but is presented glowingly, persuasively,
as the perfect path for the spiritually minded.
Be here now, as a proposal,
is certainly helpful for some sometimes,
as when lost (ruminating) in the past or future.

It doesn't help if lost, if locked, in the present —
where all thoughts of past or future
are poison to be avoided —
with no possibility of seeing
what we might like more
   than what is happening
      here and now,
   than how we are dealing with that,
      here and now.

Here, no possibility of remembering loving moments
and friendships that have changed through time,
of imagining what might bring us fulfillment in life.

Giving such power to the now does not permit us
to get an overview of our life and what is
most satisfying in it, or most frustrating in it,
or what we would find of great value
to continue, to change, to begin, or to end
at least, as *now* is usually contrasted with *then*, where
to be in this tiny *now* is to be locked in the present
with no greater appreciation of the process, the flow,
of our life than a bee of its, a bee here a limited being
with little practical wisdom, prudence, or intelligence,
with little memory and no capacity for learning,
to use an ancient example from the *Metaphysics*
   of The Philosopher, Aristotle.

Sometimes now is replaced by talk of today: there is only today;
yesterday no longer exists, tomorrow does not yet exist. As a way of

focusing us on what we can do right away, such mantras — There is only today, Be here now, and so forth — can be helpful. But of course, any such motto will have serious limitations if misapplied.

We might say that if every yesterday were actually finished at the end of the day, we would all be rather free from the laws of our world (in a Buddhist perspective, newly free of all karma at the end of each day). What we would do one day would have no continuing consequences beyond that day (and this whether we take such a universe to be wonderful, neutral, or horrible).

Looking about, we can easily acknowledge that the past is here for us, both in considering large swathes of time and in focusing in on particular days: In the West, Rome was not built in a day, but it was certainly built; the great period of time for that enterprise was counted in centuries, not in days. And there is October 14, 1066 (the Battle of Hastings), June 15, 1215 (the issuance of the Magna Carta), July 4, 1776 (the date of the signing of the US Declaration of Independence), July 14, 1789 (the taking of the Bastille prison and a key point in the French Revolution); for Tibetans, surely the date is familiar of March 30, 1959 (when the Buddhist monk Tenzin Gyatso, since 1950 the Fourteenth Dalai Lama, escaped with an entourage into India). Nowhere in the world, in our world, does the past disappear at the end of the day — that much is clear.

In the collection of verses by the Buddha, the *Dhammapada* (at verse 348), a more basic meditative point was offered. The Buddha gave no priority or special status to the now over the past or the future. The proposal was not to be here now or to be "present"; the Buddha proposed, rather:

> Let go the future.
> Let go the past.
> Let go the present.
> Be on the far shore.

The power of process transcends the power of now.

THE MOUSE

To Master Ko Bong

The mouse eats cat-food, but the cat-bowl is broken. What does this
mean?

When you see the form to be
transparent,
why stay there, feasting
on
Nothing?

GLOSSARY

Adamantine Teaching. Tibetan Buddhism, under its name of Vajra-yāna: the vehicle (yāna) that cuts sharply yet is itself indestructible, as a lightning bolt or a diamond (vajra).

anupassanā. The vision (-passanā, Skt.: -paśyanā) that follows along according to what it is seeing (anu-).

arahat, arahan. (Skt.: arhat, arhan. Chinese: lóhàn, via arahan, alahan, lahan, to lohan). Lit., a worthy one. One who has gained Awakening after hearing the buddhadhamma.

ātman. Self, taken as a constant, reified entity: the ego of *ego*tistic and of "clear *ego* boundaries."

bāla. Young, not yet fully developed. Said of a sun recently risen, a moon when crescent, grass of tender new blades, as well as of a child, the childish, the puerile. In the Indic word, the stage of development is in focus. In this way, misleadingly rendered "foolish."

bālajana. People (jana) who are bāla (not yet fully developed).

bodhi. Enlightenment, or awakening. From the verbal root budh/bodh.

bodhisattva. (Pāli: bodhisatta.) In Pāli and Theravāda Buddhism, bodhi-satta is a compound similar to "the Cheltenham train" as a train whose destination is Cheltenham, thus, the term means a being (satta) destined for enlightenment (bodhi). In Sanskrit (and Mahāyāna Buddhism), the term is understood as meaning a being (sattva) who is — or whose essence is — enlightenment (bodhi).

brahmacariyā. (Skt.: brahmacaryā.) The trip (cariyā, Skt.: caryā) toward Brahma. In Sanskrit, this has a general meaning of the career or life stage of a student, while in Hinduism, it conventionally means one who is following a vow of celibacy. In Buddhism it refers to the endeavors toward enlightenment (lokuttarasīla) and is often translated as The Spiritual Life, in contrast to living a "moral" life, which is still tied into karmic fruitions joyful or painful (lokikasīla).

budh/bodh. A verbal root meaning awaken, become conscious or alert, etc.

buddha. One who is awakened. As a proper name, *the* Buddha refers to Siddhattha (Skt.: Siddhārtha) of the Gautama (Pāli: Gotama) family or clan within the Sakka (Skt.: Śakya) people, *after* the awakening or enlightenment.

buddhadhamma. The dhamma (Skt.: dharma) or Supporting Way, or Teaching, according to the Buddha.

burning karma. The processes of experiencing our karma (Pāli: kamma, meaning action, from the verbal root kr̥/kar: do make, act) in which its nature, arising, developing, ending and manifesting in subsequent "fruit" are all gone through consciously. So called out of the heat produced in this process (energy liberated).

dervish, or darvish. One in the Sufi Order begun by Maulana Jalaludin Rumi of Balkh, Khorasan. The well-known practice of whirling incessantly for a period of time derives from the teaching carried on by this Order.

deva. Lit., a shining or bright being. A divine being. The conventional Sanskrit term for a king. From the verbal root div/diu/dy(e)u, as in divine, diurnal, dyeus/Zeus, and meaning shine, lighten up.

dhamma. (Skt.: dharma.) Lit., that which supports, maintains, from the verbal root dhr̥/dhar; meaning support, keep, hold, bear, convey, endure, contain. Used referring to that which (a) supports the world in general, as the Way (Tao) of the world; legalized as Natural Law, moralized as Duty. Or, to that which (b) supports the world as an enlightening understanding (Teaching), or as (c) the nature of something, or as (d) the various particular moments within the overall flow of reality, that is, all particulars of consciousness, whence it said, Sabbe dhammā anattā, All experiences are non-Self.

dharma. See dhamma, buddhadhamma.

dukkha. (Skt.: duḥkha.) Pain, discontent, rough times, torment.

gate, gate, pāragate, pārasamgate. From a Buddhist Sanskrit chant, continuing: bodhi svāhā (bodhi: awakening, svāhā: an exclamation such as Well said, Amen, Oh yes, Quite so), The -gate (pronounced "ga-te") in these words is syntactically either the vocative of gati (O the going) or the locative of gata (in being gone, in being in the state of).

Indic. A branch of the Indo-European Language Family. Its members include Vedic, Classical Sanskrit, Pāli, Māgadhi, Apabhraṃśa, modern Hindi, Punjābi, Marāthi, Gujarāti, and so on.

Ishq'allah. Part of the Sufi expression ishq'allah ma'abud li'llah, The Totality of Reality is the process of loving, and what is beloved, and what loves. The concept is sometimes rendered by the statement that God is love, belovèd, and lover.

Kalyāṇa. Good, nourishing, inspiring. From a verbal root, kal, meaning impel or push onwards.

kalyāṇa mitta. (Skt.: kalyāṇa mitra.) A good friend, an inspiring friend. A name for the meditation teacher in the vipassanā tradition.

kalyāṇa-mittatā-vimutti-sutta. The talk (discourse, sutta, Skt.: sūtra) on freedom (vimutti, Skt.: vimukti, release, liberation) through good (kalyāṇa) friendship (mittatā, Skt.: mitratā).

karma. See burning karma.

Karuṇa-pati. A name meaning lit., Guardian or Lord of Compassion.

Krishna/Kṛṣṇa. Lit., The Dark One, the dark-blue-skinned avatar of Vishnu. Krishna knows the senses (Go-vinda), and is the lover of Rādhā and the other cowherdesses.

lokikasīla. A way of acting (sīla) which takes place on the karmic level involving pain and satisfaction, which is, that is, worldly (lokika).

lokuttarasīla. A way of acting (sīla) which is beyond the level of merit/evil, which is beyond the worldly (lokuttara).

mahāsattva. Lit., a great being. A transcendent bodhisattva, that is, one not in human form. Hans Schumann, *Buddhism*, pp. 112-113, gives a more precise account than at either E. Conze, *Buddhist Wisdom Books*, p. 23, or at M. L. Matics, trans., *Shantideva's Entering the Path of Enlightenment*, p. 310.

Mahāyānists. Followers of the Mahāyāna Teachings, the developed thought of the Buddhist Tradition of several centuries after the Buddha (about the beginnings of the Christian Era). This term is in contrast with Hīnayāna, a derogatory term for earlier ("pristine" or "Southern") Buddhism. For more, see H. Schumann, op. cit. (just cited), pp. 91-94.

Māra. A personification of the tendencies toward unalertness or being deadened to experience. Later taken as a woman (Mārā), Māra was originally a man, the father of the three forms of stupefaction that appeared in the last watch of the night before the Buddha's enlightenment, as Mara's three daughters Ragā (Excited Desire), Aratī (Discontent), and Taṇhā (Skt.: Tṛṣṇā, Thirst, "Grabby" Desire).

Māyā. Lit., an artifice, a deceit, a fraud, trick, or illusion. In Vedānta, unreality as the illusion that there is a reality separate from and other than the Totality (or Deus-sive-Natura, or the Sufic mystical Allah).

Nāga. A hooded serpent. After the Buddha became awakened, he sat in meditation for 49 days. During this time it began to rain. A nāga wrapped itself around the Buddha and used its hood as an umbrella to shelter the Buddha. The Nāga is sometimes represented as a dragon.

Nāga-Buddha-rūpa. A statue (rūpa, q.v.) of the Buddha with Nāga.

namas-te. Lit., bowing to you. Conventionally a salutation of respect, both Hello and Good-bye, as are Aloha, Shalom, Salaam. In its deeper meaning (paramārtha) it may be glossed "I honor that within you which is beyond the superficiality of conditioning."

nirvāṇa. (Pali: nibbāna.) Popularly said to derive from nir+vā, thus meaning "blowing out" (a fire, etc.); this is its more active interpretation. Alternatively it is understand in the image of a fire burning itself out when we no longer add fuel to its process. The state free of torment and strife, nirvāna is not the same as extinction of life (see vibhava-taṇhā). Traditional commentaries such as the *Abhidhammattha Sangaha* analyse it as freedom (nir-) from desire (-vāna). The Buddha described nibbāna or nirvāṇa as the greatest happiness (*Dhammapada*, v. 203).

om. In Hindu tradition, a sound held to represent all sounds. Composed of a-u-m, it sound-wise embodies reality (since a=Vishnu, u=Shiva, m=Brahma) and so indicates in language all that is beyond language: "all that we may say here is but a pointing to what is beyond these mere words." The sound is held to have physical powers we can experience by constant repetition. (Try and test it out!)

Pāli. A Middle-Indic language (see "Indic"). Used for the preservation of the Theravāda tipiṭaka.

pāramī. (Skt.: pāramitā.) Quality brought to full development or "perfection" (its usual translation), traditionally given as six pāramitās (Mahāyāna) or ten pāramīs (Theravāda).

pārasamgate. Alternatively spelled as pārasamgaté (to show pronunciation): see gate, gate, ...

rūpa. Form, shape, physical manifestation, image, statue.

sādhu. Success! Well done! Excellent!

samsāra. The integrated (sam-) on-flowing (-sāra) stream of life. Often translated as The Wheel of Birth and Rebirth.

samyutta-nikāya. A nikāya (collection or major unit), the third of five nikāyas that together compose the sutta-piṭaka of the tipiṭaka, q.v. It appears in translation under the title *Kindred Sayings*.

sati. Mindfulness, alertness, recollectedness (Skt.: smṛti), from a verbal root smṛ, recall.

sati-paṭṭhāna. (Skt.: smṛty-upasthāna.) The (four) foundations (paṭṭhā-na, Skt.: upasthāna) of mindfulness (sati, Skt.: smṛti.) The term is also used as a name for the related practice (Satipaṭṭhāna Meditation), alternatively called Mindfulness Practice and Vipassanā Meditation.

Shiva. The embodiment (mūrti) — in the Hindu tripartite system (tri-mūrti) — of analysis, destruction, and, later, regeneration. He is also called Naṭa-rāja (Ruler of the Dance).

sīla. (Skt.: sīla, habit, custom, disposition, character, uprightness.) A customary mode of action, word, and thought, either natural (pakati-sīla, Skt.: prakṛti-sīla) or through a discipline of rules (paññatti-sīla, Skt.: prajñapti-sīla). Often translated as Morality.

sutta. (Skt.: sūtra.) A talk or discourse of the Buddha. For more see P. Yampolsky, *The Platform Sutra of the Sixth Patriarch*, p. 125, fn. 1.

tantra. Lit., a means (-tra) for expansion (tan-). That which we use to become less constricted. A practice that carries on through immersion and saturation (a gourmand of life), rather than by control and selectivity. Cf. yoga.

Theravāda. The doctrine (-vāda) of the Elders (thera-), preserved in Pāli. Also called Pāli Buddhism or Southern Buddhism, Sri Lanka having been an early home for this tradition. One among those Schools disparagingly referred to as Hīnayāna. See Mahāyānists.

tipiṭaka. (Skt.: tripiṭaka) The three (ti-) baskets or collections (-piṭaka) composing the core of the Theravāda dhamma. Consists of the Vinaya-piṭaka (Procedural and Criminal Law), the Sutta-piṭaka (Discourse Collection), and the Abhidhamma-piṭaka (Abstract Psychology).

U Ba Khin Tradition. A particular form of vipassanā meditation in which great emphasis is placed on the practice of concentrative awareness of the body, in mindfulness of the breath at the nose and in "sweeping" one's attention systematically through the body. The school takes its name from the twentieth-century Burmese vipassanā meditation teacher, U Ba Khin, who traces his tradition to Ledi Sayadaw and whose own well-known disciple, in turn, was Goenka. See further the discussion of "samathapubbangama-vipassanā" under the entry "vipassanā meditation."

vibhava-taṇhā. (Skt.: vibhava-tṛṣṇā.) The thirst (taṇhā, Skt.: tṛṣṇā) for vibhava, for the end (vi-) of ongoing process (bhava), for extinction.

vinaya. See tipiṭaka.

vipassanā. (Skt.: vipaśyanā.) The clear (vi-), immediate, intuitive seeing (-passanā, Skt.: paśyanā), free from preconception. Insight into how things are, not how we thought them to be. An appreciation that precedes any eventual conceptualizing in language, and in this way is prior to and more immediate a process than a rendering into words and concepts.

vipassanā meditation. In the Pāli language, this is termed vipassanā-bhāvanā. Literally, this bhāvanā of vipassanā is simply the effecting, producing, furthering, or cultivation (bhāvanā) of insight (vipassanā). Traditionally, two forms of insight cultivation are mentioned. In one of these, insight is preceded by a concentration of consciousness producing a mental tranquility or samatha (Buddhist Skt.: śamatha). This is termed vipassanā that has samatha going before it (-pubbangama), or samatha-pubbangama-vipassanā. See here U Ba Khin Tradition. In the other of these, the meditator (yogi) does not base the insight cultivated on a prior, distinct tranquility practice. The yogi is then called one (-ika) who has as vehicle (yāna) insight (vipassanā) that is pure (suddha, Skt.: śuddha), or a suddha-vipassanā-yānika. A later name for such a yogi is one (-aka) who has bare insight, insight (vipassanā) which is bare, simple, unmixed (with samatha practice), or sukkha (Skt.: śuṣka), meaning literally dry or waterless, as well as mere or simple. In Pāli Commentaries, this yogi is sometimes called a sukkha-vipassaka.

yoga. Lit., a yoking. That by which we discipline ourselves. A practice that carries on by control and selectivity, rather than through immersion and saturation. Cf. tantra.

BOOKS FOR FURTHER READING
on Buddhist Vipassanā Meditation and Psychology,
and on Buddhism

There are now many books that give an introduction to Buddhist meditation practice, with or without the inclusive vision of Buddhism that underlies this practice. Some books will mention mindfulness as one of eight parts of the so-called Eight-fold Path (another name for Buddhism), or the theory of mind (the Abhidhamma or Abhidharma), that would give a deeper sense to this practice and all discussions of Buddhist psychology. A search on the internet will provide the reader with many options. The following books are one place to start.

Titles of authors here (Acariya, Achaan, Bhadanta, Bhikkhu, Lama, Mahāthera, Prince, Rinpoche, Sayadaw, Thera) are not used to determine alphabetical ordering; order indicated by underlining.

Bhadanta Anuruddha Ācariya. *A Manual of Abhidhamma*. A translation of *Abhidhammattha Saṅgaha*. Translated by Nārada Mahāthera.

Atiśa [Atisha]. *Lamp for the Path to Enlightenment*.

Buddhaghosa. *The Path of Purification* (*Visuddhimagga*). Bhikkhu Nyāṇamoli (Ñāṇamoli Thera), translator.

Robert E. Buswell, Jr. *Tracing Back the Radiance: Chinul's Korean Way of Zen*.

Achaan Cha. *A Still Forest Pool: Insight Meditation* (compiled by Jack Kornfield).

Pema Chödrön. *Tonglen: The Path of Transformation*.

Edward Conze. *Buddhist Wisdom Books*.

___, in collaboration with I. B. Horner, David Snellgrove, Arthur Waley, editors. *Buddhist Texts Through the Ages*.

Dhammapāda. Translated by A. P. Buddhadatta, S. Radhakrishnan, Nārada Thera, John Ross Carter and Mahinda Palihawadana, etc.

Dharmarakṣita. *The Wheel of Sharp Weapons Effectively Striking the Heart of the Foe*, with Commentary by Geshe Ngawang Dhargye.

V. R. Dhiravamsa. *Healing through Pure Mindfulness*.

___. *The Middle Path*.

___. *New Approach to Buddhism*.

___. *Nirvana Upside Down*.

___. *Una nueva visión del Budismo*.

___. *The Real Way to Awakening*.

___. *Turning to the Source.*

___. *Unión de los opuestos.*

Gil Fronsdal. *Unhindered: A Mindful Path through the Five Hindrances.*

Mitchell Ginsberg. *Calm, Clear, and Loving: Soothing the Distressed Mind, Healing the Wounded Heart.*

___. *The Inner Palace: Mirrors of Psychospirituality in Divine and Sacred Wisdom-Traditions.*

___. *Peace and War and Peace: The Heart in Transformation.*

S. N. Goenka. *Meditation Now: Inner Peace through Inner Wisdom.*

Daniel Goleman. *Emotional Intelligence.*

___. *The Meditative Mind.*

Joseph Goldstein. *The Experience of Insight.*

___. *Insight Meditation: The Practice of Freedom.*

___. *Mindfulness: A Practical Guide to Awakening.*

__ and Jack Kornfield. *Seeking the Heart of Wisdom: The Path of Insight Meditation.*

Lama Anagarika Govinda. *The Psychological Attitude of Early Buddhist Philosophy.*

Herbert V. Guenther. *The Jewel Ornament of Liberation* by Gampopa.

Bhante Henepola Gunaratana. *Mindfulness in Plain English.*

Tenzin Gyatsho, the XIVth Dalai Lama. *How to See Yourself As You Truly Are.*

____. *The Opening of the Wisdom Eye.*

Akira Hirakawa. *A History of Indian Buddhism.* Translated and edited by Paul Groner.

Hongzhi. *Cultivating the Empty Field: The Silent Illumination of Zen Master Hongzhi.*

Jon Kabat-Zinn. *Coming to Our Senses: Healing Ourselves and the World through Mindfulness.*

U Ba Khin. *The Essentials of Buddhadhamma in Meditation Practice.*

[Tenzin Kachö Kiyosaki] Tenzin Kachö. *Precious Life: Three Points to Finding Happiness Even in Turbulent Times.*

Jack Kornfield. *A Lamp in the Darkness.*

___. *Living Dharma.*

___. *Meditation for Beginners.*

___. *A Path with Heart.*

___. *The Wise Heart.*

Wes Nisker. *Buddha's Nature: A Practical Guide to Discovering Your Place in the Cosmos.*

Ledi Sayadaw. *Manual of Insight (Vipassanā Dīpanī).*

108

Mahāsi Sayadaw. *Practical Insight Meditation.*

___. *The Progress of Insight* (with Pāli text, *Visuddhi-ñāna-kathā*).

___. *Satipatthāna Vipassanā: Insight through Mindfulness.*

John R. McRae. *Seeing Through Zen: Encounter, Transformation, and Genealogy in Chinese Chan Buddhism.*

Lama Mipham. *Calm and Clear.*

Hajime Nakamura. *Indian Buddhism.*

Thích Nhất Hạnh. *Peace Is Every Step: The Path of Mindfulness in Everyday Life.*

___. *Transformation and Healing: Sutra on the Four Establishments of Mindfulness.*

Nyānaponika Thera. *The Heart of Buddhist Meditation.*

Nyānatiloka. *Path to Deliverance.*

___. *The Word of the Buddha.*

Pai-chang. *Sayings and Teachings of Pai-chang, Ch'an Master of Great Wisdom.* Translated by Thomas Cleary.

Walpola Rahula. *What The Buddha Taught.*

___. *Zen and the Taming of the Bull.*

Red Pine, translator. *The Platform Sutra: The Zen Teaching of Hui Neng.*

___. *The Zen Teaching of Bodhidharma.*

Sharon Salzberg. *The Force of Kindness: Change Your Life with Love and Compassion.*

Śāntideva [Shāntideva]. *Bodhicaryāvatāra*, also entitled *Entering the Path of Enlightenment* and (more often in Tibetan Buddhism) *A Guide to the Bodhisattva's Way of Life (Bodhisattvacaryāvatāra).*

Hans W. Schumann. *Buddhism: An Outline of its Teachings and Schools.*

U Sīlānanda. *The Four Foundations of Mindfulness.*

Sogyal Rinpoche. *Dzogchen and Padmasambhava.*

Soma Thera. *The Way of Mindfulness (Satipaṭṭhāna Sutta and Cmy).*

Anagārika Sujāta. *Beginning to See.*

Ṭhānissaro Bhikkhu. *The Mind Like Fire Unbound.*

Thích Thiên-Ân. *Buddhism and Zen in Vietnam, in Relation to the Development of Buddhism in Asia.*

Anam Thubten. *No Self, No Problem: Awakening to Our True Nature.*

Robert A. F. Thurman. *The Holy Teaching of Vimalakīrti.*

Chögyam Trungpa Rinpoche. *Meditation in Action.*

Prince Vajirañānavarorasa. *A Comment on the Third Step of Advantage.*

A. K. Warder. *Indian Buddhism.*

Alexander Wynne. *The Origin of Buddhist Meditation.*

Philip Yampolsky, translator. *The Platform Sūtra of the Sixth Patriarch.*

BUDDHIST MEDITATION CENTERS

Beyond knowledge that can be obtained through the reading of various texts giving information on Buddhist meditation practice, with or without the inclusive vision of Buddhism that underlies this practice, it is most important and helpful to have experience ourselves in the systematic cultivation of insight through mindfulness (rendering literally the Pali name of this practice, satipaṭṭhāna-vipassanā-bhāvanā). This can give at least an initial sense of what all of this amounts to, first hand! This section suggests centers where this practice can be experienced in a residential setting, for the interested reader.

At the following centers, various teachers lead meditation workshops and retreats in which there may be significant variation in size of the meditation group, amount of personal contact with the teacher or amount of emphasis placed on ritual, on traditional vow-taking, and on Buddhist doctrine, in the number of hours of formal practice daily, or in the fees charged. And while this list is current as of the time this book went to press, it is advisable to check on specifics at the time when you are ready to experience this practice yourself.

Relatedly, in the Glossary, above, see the entries vipassanā as yoga and as tantra, U Ba Khin Tradition.

BURMA: See MYANMAR.
CANADA: Gampo Abbey, Pleasant Bay, Cape Breton, Nova Scotia B0E 2P0. *With Bhikshuni Pema Chödrön.*
    WEB SITE: http://www.gampoabbey.org
___. Tengye Ling, 11 Madison Ave., Toronto, Ontario M5R 2S2.
    WEB SITE: http://www.tengyeling.ca
___. World Dharma Online Institute & Buddha Sāsana Foundation, Attn: *Alan Clements*, 2768 W. Broadway, P.O. Box 74709, Vancouver, BC, B6K 2G4.
    WEB SITE: http://worlddharma.com
CEYLON: See SRI LANKA.
FRANCE: Dechen Chöling, Mas Marvent, 87700 St Yrieix sous Aixe (WNW of Limoges). *With Sakyong Jamgön Mipham Rinpoche, Barbara Märtens, Herbert Elsky, & others.*
    WEB SITE: http://www.dechencholing.org
___. Paldenshangpa La Boulaye, Château de Plaige, 71320 La Boulaye (SW of Beaune, NW of Mâcon, W of Chalon-sur-Saône).
    WEB SITE: http://www.paldenshangpa-la-boulaye.com

___. Lerab Ling, L'Engayresque, 34650 Roqueredonde (SW of le Caylar, via les Rives and Romiguères, WNW of Montpellier).
WEB SITE: http://www.lerabling.org
GREAT BRITAIN: Buddhapadipa Temple, 14 Calonne Road, Wimbledon, London SW19 5HJ.
WEB SITE: http://www.buddhapadipa.org
GERMANY: Haus der Stille, Mühlenweg 20, 21514 Roseburg (E of Hamburg). *With Dhiravamsa & others.*
WEB SITE: http://www.hausderstille.org
INDIA: Samanvaya Ashram, Bodhgaya 824231, Bihar.
___. Sayaji U Ba Khin Trust, Vipassanā International Academy, Dhammagiri, Igatpuri 422403, Maharashtra.
WEB SITE: http://www.giri.dhamma.org
___. Tushita Retreat Centre, McLeod Ganj, Dharamsala, Dist. Kangra, Himāchal Pradesh 176219.
WEB SITE: http://www.tushita.info
___. Dhamma Bodhi Bodhgaya Vipassanā Centre, Gaya-Dhobi Road, Near Magadha University, Bodhgaya, Bihar 824 234.
WEB SITE: http://www.bodhi.dhamma.org/
MALAYSIA: Malaysian Buddhist Meditation Centre & Wat Pinbang Onn, 355 Jalan Masjid Negeri, 11600 Penang.
WEB SITE: http://teochiewkia2010.blogspot.com/2011/07/wat-pinbang-onn.html
MYANMAR: Thathana Yeiktha, 16 Hermitage Road, Rangoon.
WEB SITE: http://www.mahasi.org.mm
NETHERLANDS: Boeddhayana Centrum, Stephensonstraat 13, 2561 XP Den Haag.
___. Boeddhayana Centrum, Vechtstraat 73, 1079 JV Amsterdam.
___. Dhammadipa Vipassanā Meditatiecentrum, St.Pieterspoortsteeg 29-1, 1012 HM Amsterdam.
WEB SITE: http://www.dhammadipa.nl
SCOTLAND: Kagyu Samyê Ling Tibetan Centre, Eskdalemuir, nr. Langholm, Dumfriesshire.
WEB SITE: http://www.samyeling.org
SINGAPORE: Buddhist Fellowship, 2 Telok Blangah Street 31, #02-00 Yeo's Building, Singapore 108942.
WEB SITE: http://www.buddhistfellowship.org/cms
SPAIN: Centro Milarepa, C/ La Naval, 167, 2°, 35008 Las Palmas de Gran Canaria, Isla Gran Canaria. *With Dhiravamsa.*
WEB SITE: http://www.dhiravamsa.com

SRI LANKA: Forest Hermitage, Kandy.
WEB SITE: http://www.nearby.lk/foresthermitage
USA (by state):
[CA]: Deer Park Monastery, Deer Park Rd., Escondido, CA 92026.
With Thích Nhất Hạnh & others.
WEB SITE: http://deerparkmonastery.org
___. Land of Medicine Buddha, 5800 Prescott Rd., Soquel, CA 95073.
WEB SITE: http://landofmedicinebuddha.org
___. Metta Forest Monastery – Wat Mettavanarm, 13560 Muutama
Lane, Valley Center, CA 92082. *With Thanissaro Bhikkhu.*
WEB SITE: http://watmetta.org
___. Spirit Rock Meditation Center, 5000 Sir Francis Drake Blvd.,
Woodacre, CA 94973. *With Jack Kornfield & others.*
WEB SITE: http://www.spiritrock.org
___. Tathāgata Meditation Center, 1215 Lucretia Ave., San Jose, CA
95122.
WEB SITE: http://www.tathagata.org
___. Thubten Dhargye Ling, 3500 E. 4th Street, Long Beach, CA
90814.
WEB SITE: http://www.tdling.org/center
___. Zen Center of Los Angeles, 923 S. Normandie Ave., Los Angeles,
CA 90006.
WEB SITE: http://www.zencenter.org
[CO]: Thubten Shedrup Ling, P.O. Box 10566, 1301 N. Weber St.,
Colorado Springs, CO 80932.
WEB SITE: http://www.tsling.org/
___. Wat Buddhavararam, 4801 Julian St., Denver, CO 80221.
[FL]: Gainsville Vipassanā Society, 5811 NW 31st Terrace, Gaines-
ville, FL 32653.
WEB SITE: http://www.floridavipassana.org
___. Tubten Kunga Center, 201 SE 15th Terrace, Deerfield Beach, FL
33441.
WEB SITE: http://www.tubtenkunga.org
[GA]: Georgia Buddhist Vihara, 3153 Miller Rd., Lithonia, GA 30038.
WEB SITE: http://www.gavihara.org
[IL]: Buddhadharma Meditation Center, 8910 State Route 83, Hinsdale,
IL 60521.
[MA]: IMS - Insight Meditation Society, 1230 Pleasant St., Barre, MA
01005. *With Joseph Goldstein & others.*
WEB SITE: http://www.dharma.org

____. Living Dharma Center, P.O. Box 304, Amherst, MA 01004. *Associated with the late Richard B. Clarke.*
   Web site: http://www.livingdharmacenter.org
[MD]: Wat Thai Washington DC, 13440 Layhill Rd., Silver Spring, MD 20906.
   WEB SITE: http://www.watthaidc.org
[NY]: Vajiradhammapadip Temple, 75 California Rd., Mount Vernon, NY 10552.
   WEB SITE: http://www.vajira.org
[TX]: Dallas Meditation Center, 727 S. Floyd Rd., Richardson, TX 75080.
   WEB SITE: http://www.dallasmeditationcenter.com
[VT]: Karmê Chöling, 369 Patneaude Lane, Barnet, VT 05821.
   WEB SITE: http://www.karmecholing.org
[WV]: Bhāvanā Society, 97 Meditation Trail, High View, WV 26808.
   With Bhante Henepola Gunaratana.
   WEB SITE: http://bhavanasociety.org

ABOUT THE AUTHOR

Mitchell D. Ginsberg, Ph.D., has been a teacher (kalyāṇa-mitta) in the Thai Buddhist Vipassanā Meditation Tradition since 1975, when he became the first Western disciple of V. R. Dhiravamsa, widely respected International Vipassanā Meditation Master, who earlier was known as Chao Khun Sobhana Dhammasudhi, when as a monk he served as Chao Āwās (or Abbot) of the Royal Thai Buddhist Mission to Great Britain, which served all of Western Europe.

For several years (1975 on), the author led Vipassanā Meditation residential workshops in Britain, France, the United States, & Norway. He was informal teacher-in-residence of the discussion group Insight Practice (a Yahoo group since 1999), and the group's registered owner and moderator from 1996-2010.

Since completing graduate studies and teaching in Philosophy at the University of Michigan in 1967, the author has held various university professorships, at Yale, the American Institute of Buddhist Studies, Antioch University, IUPS (the International University of Professional Studies), and elsewhere, teaching in departments of Philosophy, Far East Studies, and Humanistic, Clinical, and Transpersonal Psychology.

He has studied at UNAM (Universidad Nacional Autónoma de México) and at the Université de Lausanne (Switzerland) and has also held post-doctoral fellowships at MIT in Linguistics and Psycholinguistics, at The Langley-Porter Stress Clinic of UCSF Medical School (San Francisco) in Complicated Grief, a condition more recently understood within the framework of the now-widely-recognized diagnostic category of PTSD (Post-Traumatic Stress Disorder), and Visiting Scholar and Research Scholar appointments at UCSD (San Diego, La Jolla) in History, Middle East Studies, Judaic Studies, and in the UCSD Medical School's Psychiatry Department, and elsewhere.

He is author of a number of books that are listed at the beginning of this book, and has also authored articles published in scholarly journals in four countries. He has more recently also been Editor-in-Chief of the publishing house, Wisdom Moon Publishing, LLC, which he founded in 2012.

He has been a psychotherapist and family therapist since the late 1960s.

During these decades, he has used Buddhist meditative principles in his work, writings, and personal life.

Since 1982, he and his wife have lived in San Diego, where their two children were born and have grown to adulthood.

www.ingramcontent.com/pod-product-compliance
Lightning Source LLC
Chambersburg PA
CBHW020910090426

42736CB00008B/558

9 781938 459498